The
Effective
Manager

by William A. Newman

The Effective Manager

- for new and advancing managers

by William A. Newman, *Training Consultant*

© 2012 Performance Publishing Company Ltd.

ISBN:9781475017861

To

All of the managers with whom I have enjoyed working with over these many years.

Table of Contents

Prologue

All of the books in the world won't prepare a person properly for that first day – even the first few weeks as a manager. The first time we have responsibility not only for our new job, but for our people doing their jobs, it can be a rewarding thing. But the job will be even more rewarding when it is done properly and we can avoid certain mistakes.

The purpose of this book is to help new and advancing managers learn and develop additional skills to help them become more effective managers.

If you believe you can make a difference, then you probably will.

Chapter 1

A New Attitude to the Job

A New Role

Managing others can only be fully understood by those who do it. This does not mean it is mysterious, it just means it is hard to explain – like describing swimming, to someone who has never tried it. That first day on the job can be frustrating and many managers have been heard to say, "I didn't know how well off I was. At least I knew what I was doing." And there lies the problem. When we become managers, we must realize that we've taken on a new role, one for which we have the qualifications – but for which we probably have not been trained.

There was one thing about the old job – we knew what to do and when to do it. In fact, that's probably why we got our new job in the first place; we could do our job better than anyone else. Someone looked at us and decided we were pretty good at our job and seemed to have the qualities for making a good manager.

Chapter 1

So they promoted us to manager. Now we have the job, but what do we do? In the old job we were trained. We were never given a job to do and left with no more instruction than "Just do what comes naturally to you." But that's the situation right now. We have people working for us and we really can't do their work for them. Our job is to see that *they* do the work. No matter how slow they seem to be, or how bad their attitude is or how much they mess up the job, our role is to get work done by them, *not do it ourselves*.

Remember when we used to complain about the boss doing things wrong? Remember those sessions when we and the rest of the workers used to really let the boss have it behind his back? Well, we are the bosses now and they're talking about us. This means we are going to have to start looking at things differently. *Our job is to worry about the job.* This doesn't mean our people aren't important – we've already seen that they are the ones who do the work for us – but it means that we must learn to think about both the people and the job, not letting one get more important than the other. And that's difficult as will we see in the coming chapters of this book.

Let's look at a simple example. Katherine comes in red-eyed and obviously has a problem. As the story unfolds, it looks something like this:

Katherine's having family problems. She and her husband haven't been married very long and this morning they had an argument. The husband was angry and said some pretty mean things. Katherine has decided to go stay with her mom for awhile and wants the afternoon off so she can go home and pack before her

Chapter 1

husband gets home. The only thing is she can't afford to lose the pay (now that she may be on her own) and wants to come in on a Saturday and make it up. This means actually showing her time as worked this afternoon, but nothing on the Saturday she works. She is willing to work all day for the half time off so she does not lose the money. The truth is, we can't afford to let her go – even without pay – because of the heavy workload today. But, as distraught as she is, there's no telling what how she will react if we tell her she can't go. She's waiting now for an answer and needs it immediately so she can call her mother.

As managers, we are supposed to make the right decisions.

Well, what do we do? The problem is real and important to Katherine. As managers, we are expected to make the right decisions. Suppose we let her go, with or without pay: what will we tell Rachael when she comes in next Friday to do the same thing, so she can go away with her boyfriend. How will we explain to her the difference in our treatment of the two situations? Suppose we don't let her go; how much production can we expect to get out of her for the rest of the day? How will we explain the loss of production to our boss? What will our decision do to the morale in the office? Does it matter?

Chapter 1

New Words – New Meanings to Old Ones

As we go along we will see better approaches to solving this kind of problem than just doing what comes naturally. But for now, let's say that we must learn a new vocabulary. At least, we must learn new meanings for old words. They are going to be key words and key meanings for years to come. They are going to be the things that we spend our time thinking about, worrying about and making decisions about. Words like *management* take on a different look now. Also *money* and *time* aren't bad words anymore. We can't make decisions just on the basis of emotion or even on the feelings of the people involved. We make decisions on the basis of good job management. We make them in light of what's good for the organization – which *includes the feelings* of the people but not *only* the feelings of the people.

All of this says that the word *production* should take on a new meaning for us. We aren't responsible just for *things* anymore; people and money and time and production have suddenly become inseparable. And remember, the thing that we were best at – getting the job done – we are no longer supposed to do. And remember too, that we may not have been trained to do this new job of managing people. Of course, there are some basic rules: treat them as we would like to be treated; remember that they are human beings – the basic human courtesies still apply. But we may not even be sure how we would like to be treated in a similar situation. Also, knowing what we do about production needs and work scheduling and profits and the bosses' demands means that we would want to be treated differently from those who don't know about these things. And suppose we decide that Katherine and

Chapter 1

Rachael *are* human beings – so what? That's a nice thought, but what do we do with their problems now that they've become human beings. What do we do about getting the job done?

Though this may sound a bit heartless, it really isn't. It just means, that being a manager changes things for us. It changes our outlook and presents us with new problems. It changes our perspective and gives us a bigger picture to look at. It doesn't take the human element out; it puts other elements in. It gives us more factors to consider when we make decisions. It does, in fact, give us the right and opportunity to make decisions that were not ours to make before. As we said before, the *job* becomes important now, and all these other things are part of getting the job done. It doesn't make us any less interested in people; it makes us interested in them because they are the ones that make us look good or bad. They have been entrusted – in a sense – to our hands, and we have an obligation to see that things go well for them. But the job has been entrusted to us, also, and we have an obligation to the organization to see that the work is done so that *all concerned* will profit.

A Different Gang Now

The managerial role has been referred to as the lonely role. It looked simple enough when we were working for the boss and he or she was making all the decisions. It didn't seem too bad when he or she just seemed to hang around doing very little but getting in the way. As a matter of fact, we remember when we used to say, "They really have it made. We do all work and the boss gets the credit and the money and the office!" This job looked

Chapter 1

pretty easy when we were the employee. But somehow it doesn't look now the way it did then. Former co-workers look different to us now. But they haven't changed. And we haven't changed. So what's different? The *job* is different. The responsibility has changed. Our viewpoint has changed and our loyalties have probably changed too. Whether we like it or not, the people working for us don't see us the same way either. A few managers have been able to make a go of it by telling the old gang that nothing has changed. They have continued to go on break and eat lunch with them and complain about the organization with them, and knock the big boss with them and still get the work done and handle discipline problems and fire some and promote some and not get into trouble with the group – but there aren't many successes who took this route, and there are plenty of failures to show that it is a dangerous route to take. Being a regular guy is nice and it's all right, too – but only if the phrase means that even though you are the *boss*, you are still a regular guy.

The important thing is that we belong to a different gang now. We have to give up some of the pleasures of being part of the old gang and accept our position as the boss. As the boss, we belong to the gang that is made up of other bosses. We don't have to associate with them, but we have to communicate with them, on an equal level. We still have to communicate with those who work for us and on their level, too. As we look out over the group that works for us, we must say, *"We are a group that must stick together, perform as one unit and meet the organizational goals. But even though we work as one, I must be the leader. I must set the pattern of leadership by letting them be a part of goal setting; I must lead by giving them as much authority as possible so they can*

Chapter 1

*do their job with a minimum amount of interference
from me; I must see that they develop to their full
potential; I must see that their needs are met; but – I
must do these things as the boss, not as one of them."*

How do we accomplish this without being snobbish or
conceited or overbearing? It isn't easy, but it isn't
impossible. In the next chapter we will see some
examples of how it can be done successfully.

Review

The role of a new manager is quite a change from
whatever else we have been doing. Coming from within
the organization will cause one kind of problem, coming
from outside will cause another. In either case, things are
going to be different from now on. The purpose of the job
is different. Viewpoints are different. Like it or not, we're
part of a different group now; we're part of the managing
effort, rather than a part of the hourly worker effort. Our
job is to get the work done through others and not do it
ourselves. Instead of complaining about the boss, we're
the boss. Instead of complaining about the policy, we're
the ones who must implement the policy. Instead of just
waiting for someone to appraise us, we must do the
appraisal of others. This goes on and on, because we've
taken on this new role. It takes some getting used to, but
we can do it. Many have before us and they're better for
it. We will be too.

Chapter 2

A New Attitude towards the Subordinate

As new managers, one of the most difficult things for us to accept is the fact that those under us may be able to do our job just as well as we can do it. In fact, under different circumstances, one of those under us might well have been the boss instead of us. What made the difference? Brain power? Probably not. In our ability to think, most of us come out very close to the middle range, even though we like to think otherwise. The fact that we are bosses doesn't reduce the brain power of those we manage, or mean that we necessarily have more than they have. What about knowledge of the job? This varies of course, because many new managers know their former job better than anyone else – which may be the reason they were selected for the manager's job in the first place. On the other hand, as new managers, we may know less about the job we're managing than anyone else – having been promoted from some other job in the organization, or hired from the outside. Overlooking the matter of luck or influence, the only thing we can say for sure is that the new manager got the job because someone in higher management thinks that he or she can handle the job of getting work done by directing the activities of others.

Recognize Their Abilities

So what, then, should be our attitude toward those who work for us? The important thing to remember is that it is to our – and the organization's – advantage to use their talents as much as possible, leaving less and less of their job for us to do. It's rather poor management of time, people and talent to let brainpower go unused, or to let experience and knowledge of the job be wasted. And the chances are pretty good that our people will use these things or not use these things *as a result of things that we do or don't do.*

In a sense we can think of our people as being a huge storehouse of brainpower and knowledge of the job. The only catch is that we must find the right keys to give us access to this tremendous asset. Not every key will work every time, nor will every key work on every individual. We spend much of our time looking for the right keys and trying them out when we find them. All of which adds to the fun and challenges of being a manager.

Subordinates Have Needs

Those who work for us have more brainpower, job knowledge and experience and they have certain needs and anxieties that work against them for awhile, but can be made to work for us. For example, if their needs are being met on the job, then we have found a good source of motivation. On the other hand, if the needs are very

Chapter 2

strong and are *not* being met on the job, then no matter how hard we work at motivating, we aren't likely to have much success. It isn't enough to just say, "Well, I have problems, too, and I don't let it influence my performance." That may or may not be true, but in any case, we still have to recognize the problems that the employee brings to work with him. This doesn't mean we have to excuse poor performance caused by outside problems, but it does mean we have to accept the fact that the employee has those problems and that they may affect his work.

But outside problems aren't the only things that cause employees to have anxieties; there are many things right on the job that will bother them and cause them to develop additional problems. For example, just the fact that you are new to the job as manager will cause certain anxieties. The employees don't know how they will relate to you. They don't know how they will fit into your thinking. They will worry about your opinion of them and the impression you will get out of their work. They will have to start all over again competing with the others in the organization to establish a position in your esteem. These aren't necessarily large problems, but they are real and must be considered by the new manager.

Not only will employees worry about how you will see them but they will be watching you to see how you act under certain conditions. What will it be like when there is a rush job to be done? Will you be the type that puts the screws on tight, or will you just relax and not worry about the deadlines? What happens when an employee does something wrong? Will you be tolerant and just say, "Forget it"? Or will you lose your cool and embarrass him or her in front of everyone? What happens when other

Chapter 2

departments or groups interfere with your activities, or don't meet their deadlines? Will you stand up for your rights, or will you let them run all over you? Your employees want to know these things about you and will be anxious about it until these questions are resolved or until you have acted in such a way as to assure them that they don't have to worry about these things.

Ambivalence – Love and Hate

One of the strange things about being a manager is that we have to learn that it's possible for our people to love us and hate us at the same time. Perhaps these terms are too strong, but they identify the problems brought about by the phenomenon of "ambivalence." This simply means that because we represent two different things to employees, it's possible for them to feel two different ways about us.

We are simultaneously a comfort and a threat to them.

As a manager, we represent employee's means of getting ahead, of getting a raise, of solving their problems, of being recognized, of being told how to do things more easily – real security. We are simultaneously a comfort and a threat to them, so they can like us for what we do for them and dislike us for what we stand for. This shows itself in the reactions of the employees to the ways in which we give them assignments. If we just make assignments and don't give the employees much direction, they complain because we haven't explained to them how we want the job done. If we give them

Chapter 2

instructions, they may complain because we lean over their shoulders all the time and don't let them do anything on their own. Again, our job as a manager is to recognize that this phenomenon exists and to look for ways of using it to our advantage.

Bosses Are Nice People

Often we find ourselves in the strange situation of seeming to defend our "boss-hood". Very early in the game we must realize that there is nothing wrong with being a boss.

We should never feel the need to apologize for it or defend it. Every organization, at almost any level, must have someone who is in charge: the boss. For whatever reason, we are that person in this situation, and it's up to us to act the part. As a matter of fact, if we find ourselves trying to defend our job as the boss, we probably have a good indication that we aren't being a very good one – "Look guys, I hate to sound like the boss, but we've got to get this job out today."

Interestingly enough, while we may try to hide the fact or avoid it, the employees never really get over the obvious fact that we are the boss. Whether or not we act like it is our choice; they still know we are, in spite of whatever we do. This means is that we should get the work done by being the boss, not by trying to be a friend or a buddy or trying to bribe employees into doing what they are being paid to do. The problems of management arise not because we are the boss, but because we don't act like the boss, or perhaps because we exploit the job of being the boss. While we have every right to be the boss, we have

Chapter 2

no right to use this fact as the only means of getting the work done. We can't demand that the employees respect us, and although we can get work out for awhile by demanding it, sooner or later such action breeds disrespect that will back to haunt us.

One of the quickest haunting jobs occurs when we've acted this way for some time, then suddenly find ourselves in a situation in which it's up to the employees to pull our chestnuts out of the fire – and of course they may 'innocently' let our chestnuts burn. So how do we act? Later in this book we will deal with some specific behavior that has proven to be very satisfactory in setting up the right relationship between the boss and the subordinate. Right now we are just suggesting that somewhere between the two extremes of trying to hide being the boss and exploiting it, lies the happy ground of being successful at it.

We Depend On Our People

Whether we like it or not, we still must depend on our people to accomplish the long range goals of the organization. We can do only a certain amount ourselves and the more of the work we do, the poorer job of managing we're doing. Sooner or later we must get the work done with the people the organization has given us to do it with. That is why our attitude toward these people is so important. We may not think we have enough people, or the right people, or enough time or enough training, but it is still up to us as managers to get the work done with these people, at this time, under these conditions.

Chapter 2

And this brings us to another critical thought: These are also the people who will make us look good or bad. These are the people who can make or break us as managers. Our ability to use their skills, our ability to motivate them to perform, our ability to get them to think and do the things the organization wants, are the things that we will be rated on when our appraisal time comes around. So their performance will have a direct and important bearing on our rating as a manager.

They Get Our Job

Finally, our attitude toward people is important because we have an obligation to the organization to see that those who work for us develop the right attitude. It is from these ranks that our job, or others like ours, must be filled, and the way we train them, use them and treat them will determine whether or not the organization has enough properly trained managers to replace us and others like us when we move on to better things. Our attitude toward them may well determine the attitude they have toward their subordinates when they are promoted. Equally important, it may determine their attitude toward the organization as a whole, both now and when they become managers. It is just as short sighted to think of our people only in the jobs they fill as it is to think of ourselves as only in the job we fill. And it is certainly a reflection of us if we have failed to develop anyone under us who is capable of handling much, if not all, of our work when we are away from the office or when we moved to another assignment.

Chapter 2

Review

What have we said about our attitude toward our subordinates? We have said that we must realize that they have a storehouse of brainpower and experience for which the successful manager will find the keys. It is through the abilities of the subordinates that the job must get done. We've seen that the subordinates have certain needs and anxieties that they brought to the job or that may have developed after they got there. In fact, we are part of the problem, because we represent both a threat and a source of security to them. In the process of getting the job done, we've got to be careful not to try to defend being the boss. We don't need to defend it or hide it, but we don't want to exploit it, because the people who work for us are the means by which the organization will meet its objectives. These are the same people who will determine to a large degree just how well we do when we are appraised, because our job is really one of getting the work done through them. Finally, these are the people who should be able to move into our job when we are moved on to other jobs. Our attitude toward these people will largely determine our actions toward them; hence it will determine how well they are able to take over when we leave.

Chapter 3

A New Attitude towards the Boss

Bosses Have Their Own Problems

One of the things that confront us soon after we become managers is the fact that our problems are often compounded by our own people coming in with their problems, which gives us less time for our own. This really ought to be a very loud message for us: If it's true for us, it must surely be true for our boss. In fact, it is very true. Even though we don't like to admit it sometimes, the boss is usually working on problems of greater magnitude than ours. In a sense, our problems are really our boss's too and so are all of the problems of the other people who work for him or her. Even if our boss hasn't got more important problems, he or she at least has more. It makes sense that then, to avoid adding our problems to our boss's burdens, or at least not adding any more than we can help.

Chapter 3

The thing we want to do is make very sure that we understand the boss's role and our own role, and where the dividing line is between them. We need to remember that just as it's our job to get a certain portion of the work done through other people, so it is the boss's job to get things done through us. If we get the idea that the boss is just sitting around giving us work so he or she won't have anything to do, let's stop and realize that our people may feel the same way about us.

Another thing to remember is that since our boss has the responsibility for our decisions – as well as the decisions of his or her other subordinates – any bad decisions he or she makes have more important results than ours would. This doesn't mean that we can forget about using good judgment, or that our boss is going to check everything we do anyway, so why worry about doing it right. It means just the opposite; it means that the better judgment we use, and the better job we do, the better job the boss can do. We help our boss handle the bigger, broader problems with better judgment because we have bought him or her a little more time. And the better our boss does, the better the final results will be for us. Even if we don't get the credit for a job well done, we are still in the group that got the good results and it will pay off in the long run.

Bosses Have Feelings Too

Most training we will get as new managers will tell us that our people have feelings, anxieties, problems, needs, etc..., a fact we all readily agree with. But sometimes the implication is that we as bosses don't have any feelings or

Chapter 3

problems, or at least that we aren't supposed to let them show. Actually no one argues that bosses don't have problems, and most will agree that we need to be careful about letting these problems affect our behavior. Even so, we have to admit that they do show sometimes. We can't help it, perhaps. But wait – if we admit that we have feelings that show some- times, shouldn't we also admit that our boss must also have problems and feelings that may show in his or her behavior from time to time?

As a matter of fact, our boss has just about every problem and anxiety that we might have: worries about home, family, money, chances for promotion, relationship with the others on the same level, and whether or not he or she is being a good boss. And of course, like ourselves, our boss is concerned about the relationship with his or her own boss. We're kidding ourselves if we think we have a monopoly on problems, either personal or professional.

We tend to forget that the boss has a boss too. As much as we'd like to think that our boss always worries about us first, we'd be more honest to admit that we don't even do that for our people. When the going gets rough around the office or plant, we can't help but think, "How's this going to affect me?" We don't start to worry about those under us until after we've answered that question. So it is with most bosses, including our own, most likely. But that's all right, as long as we recognize that our boss is only acting human, and is reacting about the same way we would under similar circumstances. That's no excuse for our boss to treat his or her people wrongly in such situations, but at least we recognize the reason for the behavior and so may know how to act in return.

Chapter 3

The Boss Is One Step Removed

One problem that confronts our boss is that of being one step removed from the job and activity of our people, just as we're one step removed from our boss's boss. This means there's a chance our boss is not getting a full view of the situation, just as we may not be seeing things from the same angle as he or she does up the line. The chances are pretty good that our boss won't see things the same way we see them, especially about our people and their work.

Our boss must see all of this through the information we provide and from personal observation, then relate it to the bigger organization picture he or she is looking at. Also, our boss has certain charges from his or her boss, certain objectives that he or she has set, and other people to worry about besides us and our people – all of which cause him or her to see things quite differently from the way we do. So there shouldn't be any great mystery if our boss's interpretation of these things differs from ours.

Take the matter of appraising our people. Being one step removed, our boss may fail to see the potential we see in some of our people. He or she may be judging them on past performance and fail to realize how well they are developing. Since we see them every day, we have a much better chance to see how they develop and how much better they handle responsibility than they did a few weeks ago. Our boss's opinion of the person we have in mind may be based on past performance that created an unfavorable impression, so our boss can't believe that there has been a change. By the same token, our boss may find it hard to believe that a person isn't performing as

Chapter 3

well as he or she should be. We may have an employee who was rated as satisfactory at one time but for some reason is not just performing up to the standard we expect. Our boss may be dubious about our evaluation because the previous record doesn't bear us out. To make matters worse, since he or she must base a judgment on less information than we have, our boss may form opinions on incorrect information or even for emotional reasons. He or she may base an opinion on something overheard on the elevator or something heard about the employee through some one else. While such information is not reliable, it may be all that our boss has, especially if we have failed to keep him or her properly informed. We all form opinions based on the information we have to work with – the boss is no exception.

We Are One Step Removed, Too

The boss isn't the only one who is apt to form opinions on limited amounts of information. We too, are often guilty. We must be careful not to pass judgment on policies too quickly, before getting the whole story. Policies that are set one or more steps above our boss will likely lose some of their meaning and reason for existence by the time they get to us. Not only that, but the boss sees them in relation to his or her job and subordinates; we see them in relation to our job and subordinates. Each of us has a particular window to look out of, so each sees something a little different from what the other sees.

Policies that are not fully explained may appear to be unreasonable. When we fail to get the whole picture, we may say that the organization is making bad decisions. If

Chapter 3

we don't know all the facts, we just don't see things as we should. Does this mean that the boss ought to tell us everything that he or she knows and the reasoning behind every decision that is made? Of course not, although we often act as though we expect it. At some point we need to develop enough confidence in the boss and the organization to realize that they are making decisions on the basis of more and better information than we have. If we still have doubts, then we should try to find out more about the reasons behind what is happening. This is the place to request the information, though, not demand it.

The boss is obligated to help us as much as possible, but not to spend all his or her time trying to justify everything the organization does. We wouldn't want our people using up our time in this manner. We should make an effort to tell our people as much as we can about the rationale behind policies. But this doesn't mean that the only way to motivate our employees is to spend most of our time defending and justifying the organization's policies.

One problem we have as a new manager is that we are sort of starting from scratch in finding out just what the organization's goals really are. Because we are new, we naturally are missing quite a bit of background on why the organization does certain things in certain ways. This will cause a hardship on us because we may find ourselves going off in the wrong direction without even realizing it, then having to reverse ourselves and perhaps lose face in doing so. There aren't many orientation programs that will bring us up to date on all the things we need to know about the background of the group, the department and the organization as a whole – so we must

Chapter 3

hit the ground running to catch up. We can't just sit back and say, "Well, now that I'm a manager, it's up to the organization to train me in all the things I need to know." When we accepted the job as manager, we also accepted the responsibility for a large amount of our own development, including finding out about how and why things are run the way they are. The task is a difficult one, but it must be accomplished if we are to make a success of the new job.

Making Their Job Easier

One thing as new managers that we should get into the habit of doing is making the bosses' job easier by being good subordinates. How do we do it? It's a lot easier than we think. All we have to do is imagine that we work for ourselves, then ask, "What kind of employee would I like to have working for me?" The answer to that question gives us a standard to work and live by as a subordinate. Let's look at some of the things most of us would really like to see in our employees. From this list we can make up our minds what we now have going for us, and what we should change to be better.

Supportive. We talk a lot about loyalty, but all we're really saying is that we want the people who work for us to be supportive of the organization and of us as we try to carry out the policies and procedures of the organization. We should be just as supportive of our bosses. The boss is passing down policies that he or she probably didn't set, and maybe didn't even have much input into. Our first reaction should be, "How can I see that the boss gets these policies carried out?" It isn't that the boss is always

Chapter 3

right. It's that we want what's best for the organization; and as long as we work there, we should try to support it. That usually means doing as well as we can what the boss asks us to do. Our loyalty, then, is to the organization first, the boss second, our own people third.

Positive. We all like to have positive people around us, especially working for us. Our boss is no different. We should maintain the position that what the boss says is right until it is proved wrong. We should first react in a positive way, assuming that what we are asked to do, and what we are asked to tell our people make sense. We assume that somebody knows what they're doing, even if on the surface it doesn't appear so. We like our people to assume that we have reasons for what we are doing; our bosses deserve the same treatment.

Good Work Habits. If we don't like people who come in late, leave early, take too long for breaks, or stay out too long for lunch, there's a good chance our bosses feel the same way. So, we take a good look at our work habits and try to become what we want our people to be. There's more to it than just being on time. There's the matter of being neat, avoiding untidy workstations and bad work habits.

Willing and Eager to Learn. Imagine the employee who comes to us whenever he or she doesn't understand something, or when something is going on that we haven't trained our people on. Imagine how nice it is when one of our people shows a willingness to spend time learning something new, even something that isn't an immediate part of the assigned job. Thinking about this should cause us to want to learn as much as we can about

Chapter 3

the job, even before the boss asks us to. We should be "on the door step" waiting eagerly to learn a new process – with a positive attitude that this new thing is good for the organization and we're glad it's happening.

Completed Staff Work. When we assign people tasks to do, we expect them to be done properly. We also expect them to be done thoroughly and on time. We don't like to get back unfinished or partially completed work. We like what is often called completed staff work. This simply means that the employees have gone as far as they can with the assignment. They have done everything we've asked them to do; and as far as they're concerned, what we've gotten from them is reliable and finished. So, let's do the same for our bosses. When we receive an assignment, let's determine that when we bring it back, it will be done as close as the boss wants it, it will be as nearly
Complete as we can make it.

Cooperate With Others. There is no place in any organization for bickering and in-fighting, yet we still see it. We don't like it, but we sometimes engage in it. Without thinking about it very much, we find ourselves arguing with people we work with, having small wars, being jealous over petty things, taking rumors for facts, then fighting with people about them, and cutting people down when they get a little credit that we would have liked. We do all of this without realizing that if we don't like it in our people, it's certain that our bosses don't like it either. We need to be sure that we avoid being that way, so our bosses don't have to referee our battles.

Chapter 3

Creative. If we're good managers, we like people around us who think for themselves. We admire people who are creative and use their initiative to come up with better ways of doing things, but don't get their feeling hurt if we don't agree with their every idea. Some would have us believe that there is a better way of doing everything, but doesn't mean that everything has to be done differently. We should always be looking for ways of improving the job, and should give our bosses the benefit of our thinking. At the same time, we should realize that the boss cannot and will not accept every idea we have. Though pride in our ideas is admirable, that pride shouldn't get in the way of our job. We can't afford to get our feelings hurt every time our boss turns down a *good* idea, maybe we should just determine to come up with a better onc the next time.

Not Moody. As we've said, there is no place in any organization for people to get their feelings hurt over small things. We are all guilty. We really get upset when our people take things personally and imagine that we're trying to hurt them, make fun of them, or belittle them. Yet, we may turn right around and commit the same crime with our bosses. We get upset because the boss gives a good assignment to another manager, we pout because somebody got a little credit for doing something we feel was our job to do; we worry when somebody gets recognition for a job we did or contributed to. Instead of discussing our problems openly, we let them smolder. We make problems bigger than they really are, then sit around and let them burn into a full grown forest fire. We need to remember that our bosses have enough to worry about without adding to their problems with things that

Chapter 3

are more matters of personal feelings than significant problems – more imagined than real.

Altogether, we're saying that the best way to become a good employee of our bosses is to think about how we'd like our employees to act towards us. We need to remember that our bosses have the same anxieties, the same hang-ups, the same kinds of problems on and off the job as we do. Our bosses also have bigger areas of responsibilities and more problems of deeper consequence. They certainly don't need *us* as an additional problem.

Review

As new managers, we must develop the proper attitude toward our boss and his or her job. We must recognize that our boss has to worry not only about us and our job, but also about the others working for him or her. At the same time, our boss is human and will have many of the same problems and anxieties that we have, and they may show on the job. He or she works for someone else, and so is likely to worry about his or her own position in the organization. And since our boss is one step removed from our people and their work, he or she gets much less information about our people than we do, and so may reach different or even wrong conclusions about which of our people are good and which are doing well on the job. At the same time we are one step removed from our boss's manager, so we may get the wrong impressions about the policies and decisions that are made at their level. We can't expect our boss to explain every detail and every reason for every act, so we must develop confidence in those who make the policies and ask about only those

Chapter 3

things we need to know more about in order to explain to our people. Finally, we will find it hard to learn all that we need to know about the background of the organization and its people when we first become a manager. While the organization should provide as much training as possible, the responsibility is still ours to do as much self-development as possible. Because there is so much to be learned and not much time to learn it, a good relationship with our boss will go a long way toward building mutual confidence to sustain us across the gaps in our knowledge.

Chapter 4

Manager's Relations with their Coordinates

Growing Up Is Essential

It sometimes surprises new managers that there is so much bickering and infighting going on among the other managers – their coordinates. If we're smart, we'll react by saying to ourselves, "Why don't they grow up?" That's the real problem. The ability to get along in a work situation where everyone has the same general working conditions, the same boss, and the same organizational policies to work with, is a measure of our maturity. It all seems pretty ridiculous, because most of us would rather work in a situation where everyone got along with everyone else, where everyone did their job and nobody complained about anything. But that's a dream world that just doesn't exist. Do we just give in, then, and prepare for battle?

Chapter 4

Not if we want to get our job done and help the organization toward its goals. The thing that is important is that all of our ultimate goals are the same – or should be. We want the organization to prosper; goals to be met; more money to be made available so that there will be more raises and promotions. The problem is that while we may have the same long-range goals, the short-range goals seem to differ – even be opposed to one another. Each manager is assigned a task, people to do that task, money to carry out that task, etc... Each task seems different in its purpose and goals, so conflict soon arises. We each become intent on reaching *our* goal with *our* money and *our* people. Each of us has his or her own problems to solve and our own means of solving them. The conflict arises when we get so intent on our *own* problems that we lose sight of the organization's goals and problems. We resent anyone that seems to get in our way while we are striving to get where the organization wants us to go.

We forget that the organization wants us to get there *together* with the other managers, not with their bodies strewn out behind us.

Get The Job Done, But...

Sooner or later, someone will emerge as the leader of a 'let's get along' movement. Why shouldn't it be us? We can do our part in seeing that things run smoothly and still get the job done. We really don't have many choices in our relationships with our coordinates. We can get the job done by walking all over them, caring little for how they look or feel. Or we can get our job done by issuing statements like, "Forget about them, let's get the job

Chapter 4

done." In other words, we can just ignore the managers we are supposed to be working with. Or, finally, we can get the job done through a cooperative effort, taking everything into consideration. When we think about how ridiculous it is to spend our time bickering, it's easy to see that the last alternative is the only practical one. To get the job done over dead bodies of the ones we should be working with will produce some ghosts that can come back to haunt us. We may think we've done our job well, but unfortunately, most people resent being walked over and can get vindictive in a hurry. And when they hit back, it's usually with a much harder blow than we gave them in the first place.

Ignoring the others sometimes is very tempting. "If they don't want to cooperate, just let them go their way, I'll go mine." It seems so simple, but it rarely works. All it takes is for the boss to say, "Did you check this out with Peter?" or "Will this fit into the time slot with Brenda's project?" Now we've got problems. We've either got to admit that we failed to check it out, or admit you have communication problems with these other people or go back and take the chance of having to do much of our job over, and this time having to work with those whom we've deliberately ignored.

The matter of cooperating sounds fine, but it really isn't that easy. There are some built-in traps, for instance. We want our people to be loyal. We want them to respect us as their leader. We would like to hear them say that they work for the best group in the organization. That's great – or is it? Loyalty is fine, but it can also work against us. People often find it easier to be loyal to a small group than to a large organization, so they develop strong

Chapter 4

feelings about the work group, even refusing promotions to other groups, or being disgruntled when they are moved somewhere for the betterment of the organization. This means their loyalty really isn't to the organization, but to a manager or a group of fellow workers. This isn't necessarily bad; it just becomes bad when it causes the organization's overall goals to suffer. When our people begin to compete against other groups to the extent that there are hard feelings, or one group takes advantage of another, then it is bad.

Another problem is, that resentment builds among managers, which is often the beginning of jealously. We don't like to admit that we are jealous, but let the boss spend too much time with our coordinates, and we begin to wonder if the boss likes them or their work better than ours. Again we see the immaturity coming out. Lack of confidence will produce the same results. We may feel that we can't really compete on the performance level, so we start to look for other things to make up the difference in our relationship with our boss.

We may start a whisper campaign against a fellow manager; we may resort to infighting; we may even find ways of telling the boss that the other managers have some weaknesses. We may tell the boss about foul-ups that he or she might have missed if we hadn't brought them up. Of course, the boss shouldn't think better of us for doing such a thing, but even if he or she does, we have probably weakened our position in the organization.

One of these days we are going to find ourselves needing help from someone we have reported to the boss, or hoping that the boss doesn't find out about a mess we've

Chapter 4

made, while desperately trying to get it straightened out. At that time, we may need a helping friend and not be able to find one.

Make It Work

How do we get the job done? How do we get the cooperation that it takes to get along and get the work out at the same time? Perhaps the one word that comes closest to being the key is *communication*. The old saying, "We're usually down on what we're not up on" is just as true here as anywhere else. We need to know what's going on in the other groups and it's worth our time to find out. We'll appreciate our fellow workers' jobs a lot more if we know something about their problems and the reasons for what they are trying to do. And the same is true about their appreciating what we're trying to do – they need to know where we're trying to go, how we plan to get there, and who we have working to get us there.

We need to anticipate possible conflicts and problems before they have gone too far to be stopped. We need to get into the habit of giving out as much information as possible to those we work with. We should learn to *communicate*. When we find ourselves saying to someone, "But I told..." we're actually admitting that we don't know very much about communicating. Telling rarely is communicating. One good practice is to get into the habit of writing memos and notes to the people we work with, letting them know what projects we are working on that might need their help, or that might either complement theirs or conflict in some way. The obvious fact is that they will be in a better position to help

Chapter 4

us if they know what we are doing. Equally important, if they know something of what we're doing, they will be better able to answer questions that arise from their subordinates about our work.

Another simple habit to get into is checking in with our coordinates when there is something we don't understand about their job. If one of their employees gets sideways with one of ours, don't just go and jump on somebody. Go calmly and get some facts. We aren't obligated to start a fight whenever one of our people has a problem with someone outside our group. That's building the wrong kind of loyalty. Our people may think we're great for doing it, but we aren't really helping them, ourselves, or the situation by storming around from office to office telling people off. And remember, we shouldn't even pretend that we're 'going to get this straightened out once and for all,' implying that we will jump on somebody about this. That too, builds the wrong kind of loyalty. In the long run, our people will respect us more if we provide a smooth working environment for them, and fairly harmonious relations with the others with whom they must associate.

Avoid Learning the Wrong Thing

One more problem we have to deal with as new managers is what we do around those people who have been in the organization for a long time and for one reason or another have grown bitter. There is a sort of "bitterness syndrome" that affects some people. They don't like certain policies that affect them; they don't like the way promotions are handled; they don't like the way their

Chapter 4

raises have been coming or the amount; they feel they should be higher in the organization or should be consulted more or should be making more money. Perhaps even worse, they may see us as a threat to their own security. They may feel that the new people have a better chance than they do, so they will resent us and make life a little harder for us. Most of us can handle that, because we see through it easily enough. It's the same problem we faced in school when we had better grades than a classmate who had been considered the better student for a long time. It's like the time we outran a person in a race, when they were faster or older than we were, but for some reason on this occasion we just outran them. The people who will give us the most trouble are those who do know their jobs, who are respected for their knowledge, and one of them may even be the person we've been assigned to, to learn some of the ropes. When this person has a tainted streak or is bitter, it affects us a lot more.

What can we do about such a situation? The best thing to start off doing is to *ignore it*. Certainly we shouldn't try to correct the person or try to change their mind. To start off with, we're going to lose the argument just on a basis of experience and knowledge alone. These people will know more arguments and more ways to offset ours than we'll ever be able to handle. So we just leave that idea alone. We could try to present another side of the picture as we see it or as we've been treated, but this has the same problem. In showing us where we've misinterpreted the data, they may even 'convert' us to their way of thinking. In the beginning, the best thing for us to do is simply listen and *not respond*.

Chapter 4

Later, as we get more confidence or more facts, we might try to deal with the people who are like this – but at first, leave them alone. There is always the possibility that they're right, but in the beginning we really can't tell, so saying nothing will serve us better than anything else we do. Sooner or later we've got to stand on our own feet. We've got to come to our own conclusions about the organization, about the boss, about our particular work group, and about the specific job we're working on. The sooner we do it, the better, but we ought to make sure that it's our own thinking we're doing, not that of the older and 'wiser' heads around us. Just as they have more information, they also have more biases. At least we ought to wait until we've developed our own biases before we become bitter or start to disapprove of the way the organization is run.

Another thing we're going to do some day is to develop our own standard of behavior. We may not realize it, but at first we really don't have a standard. We act like the people around us; we ask them how we should feel about things, how we should act and even what kind of action is preferable. At some point in time we need to ask ourselves, "Is this really me, or am I still just repeating what I heard?" We need to decide for ourselves how we feel about the boss, the organization, etc... and it ought to be based on as much fact and experience as possible. Above all, *it ought to be us*.

Review

Our ability to get along with the people we work with is one test of our maturity. After all, we're all working for

Chapter 4

the same organization with the same long range goals. The advantages of having a peaceful environment to work in are obvious. We need to be careful in building loyalties, to see that they're built around the organization as a whole, not just to us or our small group. When we work with others under the same boss, we need to realize that in the long run, cooperation is the key to getting the job done satisfactorily. Cutting throats or ignoring others in our work and planning may seem the quickest way, but it lacks a lot of being the best way.

The best way is to learn to communicate – not by telling, but by being sure that the fellow workers get a memo or a email from us letting them know what we are doing and suggesting ways in which getting together might help both of us. These aren't the only times we need to communicate with them, of course. We need to talk to them about possible conflicts or problems that arise among our subordinates. But getting together should be pleasant, not an effort to build our prestige among our own people. They may think we're great but that won't help the organization in the long run. The thing that's most likely to help is for us to develop a good working relationship with our coordinates so that the situation will be better for productive work.

Chapter 5

The Importance of Good Communications

Communicating – Good or Bad?

It's easy to tell people they should be good communicators; it's much harder to tell them *how* to be good communicators. One problem is that we aren't always sure just what we mean by 'good communications.' The minister who delivers a great sermon gets a rousing support from the congregation, but when someone asks what the sermon was about, very few may be able to answer correctly. When the politician holds an audience spellbound and then they go out and vote for someone else, he or she may have failed to communicate.

Chapter 5

As managers, we are most often transmitting messages that should produce some action, change something or speak to the to the action that has already been carried out.

We might define good communicating as getting the right message to the right source in an *efficient manner*. Efficient may not necessarily mean the cheapest or quickest or the easiest, but efficient means *correct*. The reason for saying it this way is that so often we take the easy way out and just *tell* somebody something. But since memory is not very reliable, this isn't a very efficient method. Pretty soon we will find that the person we told will have to be told again, or that he or she is doing it wrong, or has somehow got the message messed up. Perhaps another word we could use is *effective*. Effective carries another implication – that the message got through and that correct results will happen. When we send a message, we should think to ourselves, "It isn't whether it *can* be understood; I must be sure that it will be very difficult to *misunderstand* it."

Four Elements In Communicating

We can understand communication better if we tear it down and look at the parts or elements that go to make up any communications effort. There are four basic elements to consider, the *sender*, the *receiver*, *the message* and the *condition* under which the message is sent. Each of these things affects the results, and the effectiveness of our communication depends on how well we take each one into consideration. For example, the most powerful speaker may have trouble when the room

Chapter 5

is too warm, or when the audience is uncomfortable in some way. This doesn't mean that the speaker can't do a better job than someone else; it means that he or she could be even more effective under better circumstances. On the other hand, when the person we're talking to really wants the information we're presenting, our presentation can be pretty poor and still get the message across. But it could get across better if we were doing a better job.

When I'm bragging to my friends while driving to the golf course about my fishing prowess, I doubt seriously that I'm getting through very much, but when I'm talking to a mother whose son I've just seen in a distant city, expect the that message will get across much better. Finally, when my son wants me to pick him up from some place so he won't have to walk home, he goes into great detail and even repeats himself to ensure there is no misunderstanding.

Note the there is a difference in emphasis on where the breakdown is, in effective communication. A different element is involved in each case. In the fishing story, the subject matter nor the environment was conducive to successful transmission. In talking to the mother about her son, the message was very important to her and she was ready to hang on every word. When my son talks to me about giving him a ride, I may not be very interested in the message, but to him it is very important. And it is very important to him as the sender that I (as the receiver) get the message. There are several things to notice here about effective communication. First there is the fact that different conditions exist when we transmit information. Next there is the fact that the sender and

Chapter 5

receiver have different degrees of interest in the subject matter. The fact is, that it is rare for the sender to have the same feeling toward the message that the receiver has. If we don't take this into consideration when we communicate, we may lose the message.

One problem we have is that as senders we always want to put the responsibility for successful communication on the receiver rather than accept it ourselves. We usually react the same way when someone fails to get what we are saying. We think, "But I told him..." The first thing we tend to think is that if the receiver had listened, he or she would have gotten the message. And that is the rationalization. We are failing to accept responsibility for taking all the elements into consideration. Did we realize that the receiver wasn't getting the message? Did we realize that he or she may not have been interested, and we should have done to stir up the interest? Did we consider that the environment might not have been the best for good communicating? Were the doors open and other listening in? Was the phone ringing? Was the receiver waiting to see the boss? Were there other distractions in the office or on their mind? Was the receiver really just tolerating our conversation, waiting for the right moment to begin his retort? Did we choose the right time and the right place to discuss the subject? Did we prepare the receiver for the discussion by making it clear what is was we wanted to discuss?

These are all important considerations and we can't pay too close attention or ignore them. What usually happens is that we probably use the same approach each time and we say things the same way regardless of the circumstances or whether the person we are talking to is

Chapter 5

interested. We wouldn't dream of approaching the boss for a raise and promotion in the same manner we would order a sandwich in a restaurant. What we should do is put all of our conversation and other types of communication into the receiver's frame of reference.

The Receiver Has a Different Frequency

We think in terms of *our* goals, *our* interests, *our* needs, *our* problems – not the *receiver's* goals, interests, needs or problems. When we communicate, we do it successfully by either tuning in to the receiver's frequency or getting the receiver to tune in to ours. It usually results in both the sender and receiver wanting the other to make the change. The sender generally has the message that needs to be transmitted, and so should accept the responsibility of ensuring that both are on the same frequency.

Perhaps one of the best things we can do before we try communicating is ask ourselves what frequency the receiver is on. What is there about this message that would make the receiver understand better? If it's important to me, why should it be important to the receiver? When we have determined what the receiver's frequency is, then we must decide whether *we* would get the message from the communication we are preparing. We must ask: "Is this the best way to get the message across to Mary? Will she really read this email? Will she read it carefully enough to see that it is meant for her or that it is a completely new policy, different from the one she is familiar with? There are plenty of cases in which important new policy changes have been put into poorly crafted emails and got completely disregarded by the

Chapter 5

time they got to the people who were supposed to use them.

Barriers to Effective Communication

This brings us to the point of looking at some of the barriers to good communicating. Take the case of someone in an organization introducing a new policy by putting it into an email to management. To an outsider, reading the message for the first time, it may appear that everything is clear and that there is no chance for a communication breakdown. After closer examination, it may show that possibly hundreds of emails go around to different managers in the organization every day, often carrying insignificant details. Those who receive them have learned through experience that if anything really important needs to be implemented, there will be a big announcement made by someone else at the same time. This means to them, "If it's really important, somebody will tell us without spending a lot of time reading useless emails." Be alert enough to catch important messages among those the receiver has learned aren't very significant.

The second barrier is the other side of the coin – sending unimportant messages. It doesn't make good business sense to send messages, if you think nobody reads them anyways. It doesn't take long to get into sloppy writing habits with this thought in mind. Equally senseless is the idea of writing just to move the responsibility to someone else's inbox: "I did my part I wrote a note covering it." This becomes an unnecessary message or perhaps a much more damaging one than none at all. This is a third barrier, if we consider that our motives weren't very

Chapter 5

honest in the first place. We aren't likely to work very hard at making a message clear if we have ulterior motives in sending it. If, what we're really trying to do is hide the truth, what better way than in an incomplete message.

And even when we have the best intentions we run into another barrier: overkill. It's so important that everyone gets the message that we go into too much detail or give too many facts. As a result, the real message gets covered with background information that should have stayed in the background. The problem comes when we start to sell the idea instead of giving out the necessary information. When we start selling, we almost always go too far, often raising questions in the receiver's mind about things that aren't really important to the subject we are discussing. It's usually better to give too little information than too much. Too much not only raises questions, but may get the receivers to think about something that they are particularly opposed to, or about which they have already made some kind of judgment. When they get to thinking about that, the real message is going to suffer and probably get lost. Trying to get it across the second time will be much harder than the first time.

This suggests another barrier to good communication, the matter of organizing the message. If we hide the message among unnecessary information, it can't help but get lost. Also, if we organize it so poorly that the receiver gets confused trying to find out what we're really trying to say, we should not have sent out the message in the first place. It makes sense that the more time we spend getting to the important point, the easier it will be for the receiver to lose interest. One of the ways we can

Chapter 5

organize better is to get the important part of the message out quickly. Start off by saying what it is we are trying to get across, "This is to recommend that we proceed with the project outlined below," or "Effective tomorrow, the salary structure is being changed." The experts tell us that we remember longest, the first and last things we hear or read. This means that the closing shot at the receiver should also contain a summary or a conclusion.

In another chapter we will deal specifically with writing, but for now let's look at one of the ways this barrier works against most letter writers. When we write a letter we offer answers to problems, give out necessary information but then instead of just stopping we look for some way to end it. Usually we use some kind of over-used phrase that sounds impersonal. 'If we can be of further assistance to you in this or any other matter, please do not hesitate to call us." If it's true that we remember the first and last thing we read, then what will the reader remember about us? They may remember that yes, we are willing to help out, but we are very unfriendly and use form letter phrases to send our messages. If there is nothing friendly and helpful by the time we get to the end of our letter, the reader isn't likely to believe it just because we use some worn our phrase.

One more barrier is the matter of trying to communicate with people who have different ideas or opinions. This difference can cause the message to be lost or confused before it does its job for us. For example, when we talk to our subordinates about something the company wants, we have to remember that their views of the company are quite different from ours. We have to realize that they will likely receive the message as meaning something else if we put it terms of 'the company'. Education, experience and other factors will play a big part in our ability to communicate and are part of this same barrier. The employee who is struggling to make a mortgage payment, isn't likely to get the message that the company's new long range savings plan is a good investment at this time.

Application

Let's look at how some of these barriers work in real life. Take the matter of hiding the important messages among the less important ones. Let's consider the manager who has a large number of people working for him or her and occasionally finds it necessary to get specific messages to the group as soon as possible – but is unable to call large group meetings due to the nature of the job. A particularly important policy change has come up and it is necessary to get it to the people as quickly as possible. The choices are: (a) call the people into small groups until all of them have been covered, (b) send out a blanket email to all of them, (c) appoint team leaders to come in and get the message and then they take it to the rest of the group, or (d) post the message on the plant bulletin board next to the lunch room. Which is the wisest choice?

First, let's make sure we understand that in management there is often no clear right or wrong. There are advantage and disadvantages, and the decision really depends on which has the fewest drawbacks. So how do we get the new policy matter to the employees? Let's see what happens if we choose (d) and put the message on the bulletin board inside the plant. If the board is like many, there is a clutter of other information on it. This option has drawbacks as it gives no guarantee that all

Chapter 5

employees will see it. If we choose (b), having a blanket email sent out, this has the advantage of most people getting the message at the same time, but unfortunately not all of the employees have a company email account. There are likely to be questions and people will be discussing it amongst themselves and a miscommunication can occur. Maybe the best choice is (c), calling in a small group of team leaders to brief them and then they go out and brief the rest of the employees.

There are some real advantages to this idea, even though it sounds like it would take the same amount of time as calling in all the people in smaller groups. The advantage of (c) is that we will have a chance to sell the leaders: then they will be doing the selling of the new policy to the rest of the employees. In the long run this may work best, but the danger of having the employees get the wrong message is significant as the message will be coming from several people instead of one.

This can be corrected by having the team leaders advise that there will be group meetings later where questions can be asked. If we do a good job briefing our leaders, our work is reduced considerably. The final choice is (a), do all the briefing ourselves. If we think there will be any problems about the group accepting the policy change from one of their own members, then we shouldn't hesitate to call the small group meetings and get the policy across as best we can.

Let's look at the idea of 'over-killing' the message. We have decided that a certain idea suggested by one of our employees is a great one and we want to pass it up the line to higher management. In an effort to prove what a

Chapter 5

great idea this is we decided it would be well to give some background information on both the employee who came up with the idea and the need for idea itself. We want to do a good job of presenting both the employee and the idea, so we really lay it on thick. Of course the results are obvious – we oversell, and by the time the people who might have been interested finish going through all of the non-essentials, they have lost interest and we have lost an opportunity to sell a good idea and do a favor for a deserving employee.

How Can We Improve Communication

So far, we have talked about the barriers and other things that might hinder us from getting the message across. What are some of things we can do to really get the job of communication done effectively? First we must get the message straight ourselves. After all, it was only an idea in our mind when it all started. It wasn't full grown and it wasn't in any shape to be transmitted to anyone else. But if we go straight ahead and start explaining it without properly thinking it through, we're in for trouble.

The next things we can do, is to try and *sell* the idea. The fact that we think it is a great idea doesn't necessarily mean everyone else will agree, especially since they probably have a few ideas of their own. Just trying to force our ideas down someone's throat isn't likely to get us very far. Another thing to do is to get the message out in the open. We sometimes try to sneak an unpleasant idea between two pleasant ideas. The end result may be that we were successful – at least successful in hiding the idea. There's nothing better than tact when it comes to handling unpleasant messages – we should use it and

Chapter 5

whatever other human relation tools we can – but in the end we must make sure the real message stands out and get's recognized.

If we want to correct some behavior in our employees such as lateness, sloppy work, poor communication, bad attitudes or anything else, we'd better be sure that they know these are the things we are talking about. The situation may even be unpleasant, but at least the message will not get lost.

Next we should make certain the message gets there. It's not enough that we know what we plan to say. It's only successful communication when the message gets to the receivers. How will we know that? We will only know for sure when we hear them tell us what's been said. We want to know how they hear the message, what it meant to them and they have interpreted our remarks.

Successful communicators have different ways of getting this feedback. Some will simply ask the person they are speaking with what they have heard. This tends to put the responsibility on the listener, but it is effective. Others may ask the person to give them some feedback because they aren't sure they're communicating the message effectively. This keeps some of the blame for the potential of misunderstanding on the communicator. Still others try to get their feedback in the form of results from the message sent. They'll ask the listener what action is required as a result of the message they heard. As the sender hears certain action plans, he or she will know exactly what the listener heard and how it was understood.

Chapter 5

Whatever way we get it, we must be sure that we don't rely just on our own confidence in ourselves as communicators. We may be good, but we can be better and there is also the fact that we may not communicate as well with certain people with certain messages as we will with others.

Listening is a skill.

The third part of good communicating is the ability to *listen*. Listening is a *skill*. It must be learned and it can be forgotten even after we have learned it. Of all the skills of communicating, listening is the hardest to learn and the hardest to consistently practice.

The more we communicate, the more likely we are to forget using this skill. We get so used to hearing our own voice and saying things that sound good to *us*, that we can forget that everyone isn't always tuned into our voice or message. Listening is more than just being quiet. It means we listen for content, we listen for meanings, we listen to see if our message has gotten through. We must try not to get into the habit of hearing what we want to hear instead of what is really being said. When we are doing a good job of listening, we don't interrupt people or jump in at the end of their sentence with a quick response. We pause, if necessary, until we've processed the information we've just received. We repeat the statements or facts if we have any doubt about whether we heard right. We can ask for clarification if there's any chance of our misunderstanding something. Of course,

Chapter 5

we don't do this all the time. But we don't hesitate to do it if there's room for doubt. We learn to effectively use such phrases as, "Do I hear you saying…" and "Let me see if I have this straight…" Again, we don't use these expressions all the time, but we aren't afraid of admitting that we may not be getting all that's being said.

Finally, we can summarize these skills in this way. They've been classified as the skills of good communicators:

> Knowing the message
> Knowing that the message got there
> Listening

Remember that these are skills. They have to be learned and as we move up in the organization we tend to fade on the first one: *Know the message.* We see ourselves as well informed and because we have communicated a lot in our lives, we naturally consider ourselves to be really good at it. So we stop listening and that means we've lost any chance for good feedback. In the absence of feedback, we only have our knowledge of the subject to rely on and we may not be as good as we think we are.

The key: *We can always be better at communicating.*

Review

Much has been said about communicating. In fact, it's the 'much saying' part that has made communicating so hard to do. There is a lot more talking going on than there is listening and there is a lot more talking going on than is being understood. Most people don't realize that they are

Chapter 5

poor communicators and even blame others for not understanding what is said. Because there are always at least two people involved in any communicating effort, there is the problem that each can blame the other, with neither accepting the blame. The solution to good communicating is neither simple or something that can be done overnight. There are skills involved and these skills are often difficult to learn. The best solution is for the manager to develop some ways of checking how he or she communicates, so that at least one person in the communicating effort will be aware of the problem. Let's review: Know the message, know that the message got there and listen. The listening is the most difficult part to learn, but it is the most valuable part of the three. It is through listening that we get the feedback that tells us whether the message got there. If we aren't very good at getting the message through, the knowledge that it didn't make it through at least gives us a chance to try again.

Remember – we have two ears and one mouth, so we should try to listen twice as much as we talk!"

Chapter 6

Setting up the Work - Planning and Organizing

As we have already seen, our job as managers is to get work done through other people. We are doing our best work when we deal with the problems of getting the job done properly, rather than doing the job ourselves. While we have the direct responsibility for the employees and how they do their work, we still are not supposed to do the work ourselves.

Everyone above the worker level has some managing to do. The only difference between the front line manager and the head of the organization is the scope and responsibility of their managing assignments. Basically, every manager, has four managing functions to perform:

- Planning
- Organizing
- Directing
- Controlling

Chapter 6

The first two we'll discuss in this chapter, the last two in the next. While all managers have all of these functions, the extent in which they do them usually depends on their level within the organization. Top executives will probably spend most of their time planning and organizing, while front line managers will devote most of their time to directing and controlling the activities of people. Since all managers have all of these functions, let's look at what they *really* mean to the new manager.

Planning

First, let's be sure we understand something about all of these functions. Each is something that is done along with the job. The chances are pretty good that we'll do some of each one whether on purpose or by accident. When we talk about planning, we're talking about the everyday job – how it's done, what will be done tomorrow and where we hope to go from there.

Planning is by far the most important of all activities we've listed because everything else results from it. It is simply the means by which managers decide in what direction they want their group to go. The process can be carefully done or it can loosely. The interesting thing is that even *doing nothing* will still produce a result. The organization will still exist, tomorrow will still come and the employees will do something, right or wrong. Most experts agree that planning is the most important of all functions but the organization will not stop because we fail to plan, but it will struggle.

Failure to plan is planning to fail!

Chapter 6

Another reason for the importance of planning is that it's much harder to correct the results of poor planning than do it correctly in the first place. The results of poor planning can be disastrous and unfortunately for the new manager, they usually show more quickly for him or her than for higher management. When top management makes a mistake, it may take months or even years for it to surface. When the front line manager makes a poor plan it may be a matter of hours before the results are obvious. If an executive decides to spend more money on advertising to boost the sales of a certain product, it may take a year to see whether the campaign was a success. If a manager plans his or her work force incorrectly and has too many people off during a peak production period, the resulting slowdown will be known before the day is over.

How and What to Plan

How doe we as managers plan our work? Obviously we want to consider whatever alternatives are available to us and select the best one. Too often we think of planning as deciding what to do or what not to do. Good planning always takes into consideration all of the possible alternatives, weighs them carefully, then selects the one with the most merit. There is a caution here – *Don't* try to find the perfect solution, or the one with no drawbacks. *There rarely is such a plan.* In fact, we may have to settle for the plan with the fewest drawbacks, because none of the plans is completely satisfactory.

We form our plans by making four basic decisions:

What is to be done?
Who is to do it?

Chapter 6

How is it to be done?
When is it to be done?

Now let's take these one at a time and see how they fit into the everyday job.

What is to be done? We should have this definitely in mind before we go on to any of the other questions. For example, it isn't enough to decide that we are going to give the people some more training, then go out and find someone to do the training. We must first decide exactly what training is needed, how much we can do ourselves, how much can be done by someone else and how much can just be left undone. If we aren't careful, we'll find ourselves trying to carry out plans that weren't very definite to start with; this will result in a lot of wasted time trying to make something work that didn't have a very good start. The rule here is to be sure that we know exactly where it is we're going before we start to go there. It isn't necessary to write all of our plans down, but it sometimes helps us understand what we are going to do if we record in a memo, a positive statement of just what exactly what we plan. The plan may change as we go along, but at least we have something to change. Otherwise we will end up making our plans as we go along, changing things, repeating our errors and making a mess of things.

Who is to do it? Part of good planning is to determine whether this is a project for the whole work group, just for a few of them or one individual. If it is a one-time job, there is a great advantage in having only one or a few people work on the project. It's easier to keep up with a special project if only a few are involved and less training.

Chapter 6

time is required. If the work requires a regular responsibility of our work group, then our planning should include deciding how soon we want everyone to learn the new work.

There is an important training note here: If we aren't careful, we may let a job just gradually get done with little training of the people and the result is that the job is not done very well. We may think that one of these days we'll do the training, but we keep putting it off until a more convenient time – which never comes. A basic fact to remember about training is that like everything else on the job it must be *planned for*. The effective manager plans for it to happen.

How is it to be done? Once a goal or objective has been decided and agreed on, we still have to decide how it's going to be met. This decision has to be considered at every level, but especially at the front line level. Policies about the work will be set at a higher level. The decisions about the actual work are usually made at the point in the organization where the work is to be carried on – the front line manager. The decision may not always be made here as some managers *give up* authority to their bosses. Then they complain because they don't have enough authority to carry out their jobs, when in reality they didn't use it when they had it.

Policy setting is sometimes done unconsciously, because we can set the policy by *doing nothing*.   If we don't come up with firm policies on matters such as overtime, safety, time off, promotions or appraisals, precedents will begin to set the policies for us. If we intend to do a job

Chapter 6

without adding employees, we may be setting a policy for more overtime as we get close to finishing the job.

When is it to be done? The final question to be decided has to do with one of the most important ingredients in successful planning – time. While the most obvious conclusion is that the completion date is the most important consideration in time, this is only part of it. No deadline is missed by surprise. Long range plans usually fail because of poor short range planning. As front line managers, we are rarely directly involved in the long range objectives of the organization, but we are often very much involved in the short range plans. Meeting these short range objectives is the most important 'time' aspect of our role in planning.

Understanding the Plan

No plan is very good if it isn't understood by those affected by it. We tend to blame someone else when a plan begins to go sideways. The first thing we should investigate is whether or not the planning included safeguards against misunderstanding the plan. Were the employees informed? How ere they informed? Were they just told or did they get an opportunity to ask questions or seek additional information to get familiar with what was expected of them? This may sound like something that would only be undertaken when starting a major operation, but it is not. The employees need to know what's expected of them, even in a small one-hour project. Our people are more interested in the day to day activity than in long range operations, so it's the smaller things that are more important at this level.

Chapter 6

Who's Watching the Clock?

Something that should concern us as managers is the fact that since higher management is interested in long range objectives, they usually aren't watching the short range objectives nearly as much. This means they may not do more than read an occasional progress report with an eye on the final completion date. If we as front line managers aren't careful we may be the only ones watching the short range dates. However, we can be sure that a lot of people will be watching when it's too late to do anything about it.

Sometimes at the front line we may get the perception that everyone is watching everything and that we're just insignificant little worker bees in a giant hive. But once we've been trapped by this thinking, we're headed for trouble, especially with short range plans. Even though everyone seems to be watching over our shoulder, they still expect us to watch the day to day progress of the work. If the long range objective is to reduce absenteeism, higher management will be concerned with monthly or quarterly reports, but front line managers must worry about who shows up and who doesn't *every day*.

Objectives and Policies

Planning then, is a function of management in which we are concerned with the future of the organization in those operations for which we are responsible. In the process of planning, we decide where we are going and how we intend to get there. Usually, we call "where are we going" – *the objective* and "how to get there" – *the policy*. Some have compared this to a ship taking a trip. The objective

Chapter 6

is the destination of the ship, while the policy is the course the ship must take to get there. In a sense, the planning is the rudder steering the ship. The manager doing the planning controls the ship and with out planning, the ship has no rudder.

While it won't be dealt with in detail in this chapter, we should learn quickly that the more we take our people into the planning effort, the more likely we are to reach the objective. Since we are more likely to be involved in short term planning, we are setting short term objectives, often with short term policies. These may be day to day type things that our people know as much about as we do. Getting them to assist in setting deadlines is a good way to also get commitment to these deadlines. Getting them to participate in laying the ground rules is a good way to motivate them to work according to those ground rules.

A Brief Word about Controlling

In the next chapter we'll talk in detail about the function of controlling. We need to mention it here because planning and controlling are very closely associated with each other. A manager controls according to the planning that has been done. For example, budgeting is a type of planning that has to be done, but the budget itself is a control. While it is being prepared, the budget is part of the planning process. Once the operation has begun, it becomes part of the controlling function.

Other examples might be quality control or service standards. Determining the organization's policies on quality or service is a basic part of *planning*. When those policies go into operation, they are actually *controls*. The

Chapter 6

importance of all of this is that we should be happy that budgets, standards and controls exist, because it is through them that the desired end result is reached. They will guide us on the path and tell us when we've reached the objective, but also give us a standard to measure against along the way.

Time Management

It wouldn't be appropriate to have a discussion about planning without dealing with one of those things that needs the most planning – *our time*. One reason for planning is to help us make better use of our time. We will not do a very good job of making use of our time if we don't plan for its use. We waste our time doing things that we shouldn't do and we don't have a good way to prevent others from using our time to get their work done. Let's look at some of the problems around us that are related to time and we'll see that good planning can eliminate some of these problems.

As we spend more time in management, we see more and more things that waste our time. The list seems to endless, as we can see below:

No deadlines set	Procrastination
Cluttered work space	Surfing the web for personal reasons
Daydreaming	Poor email routing
Poor self-discipline	Poor email handling
No clear objectives	No priorities
Inability to say no	Poor priority setting
Failure to delegate	Poor work organization

Chapter 6

Underestimating others	Leaving tasks partially done
Overestimating others	Attempting too much

This list could go on and on, but we can see that many things use up our time – most of them our own fault. A brief look at the items above shows us that these are all things that *we* could and should control.   There are other types of time wasters, that aren't on this list, that have to do with outside forces which we may have no control over. We'll talk about these 'external' forces later. The 'internal' forces are the things that we usually have the opportunity to control. The failure to control them may be a lack of knowledge of how, a lack of skill in doing it or just our failure to realize that they are wasting our time.

For example, if we fail to delegate, then we end up doing things that others *could* be doing and possibly *should* be doing. We may feel it's not necessary to delegate that particular thing because we can do it quicker and thereby save time. As we'll see later, in an upcoming chapter, that's a problem of many new and experienced managers. We'll see that when we do something others should be doing, it always costs us time in the long run. But we may not know how to delegate and get the results we want. Our problem may be in not knowing what to delegate or to whom the project should be delegated. The end result is that we do it ourselves and waste time.

Let's look at some of things that researchers have found to be the major causes of poor time management. One of the major problems is that we attempt too much. There are number of causes for this problem. First, we may not

Chapter 6

know how to say 'no' when somebody asks us to do something. They come to us with a weak story, a pleading or a demanding approach and we fall into the trap of agreeing to do the job ourselves. How do we avoid this trap? There are several ways. First, we may have to take a more assertive approach in dealing with people. We should remember that every time we take on a project that someone gives us, we're saying that we would otherwise be doing isn't as important as what these people have given us. We're saying that we aren't as busy as they are. The obvious result is that they will keep giving us things to do instead of doing it themselves.

Another thing we can do to get out of the "can't say no" syndrome is to get into the habit of offering alternatives to the person who asks us to do something. We can suggest some better ways, some other people, some short cuts, maybe even some ways of eliminating the work or cutting down on it.

We can apologize for not doing it, but only if we feel some obligation to do it. We have no reason to feel guilty for not doing something that isn't ours to do in the first place. If we don't want to do the assignment, if we aren't supposed to do it, or if the person asking us could do it just as well, perhaps the best thing for us is to simply say no. It is important for us to establish the fact that we have things to do and that we already have something to do and that it is a serious thing for us to take on another project. We must learn to establish the fact that we have things to do and that we have our work planned so that *we* know whether or not we can take on another assignment.

Chapter 6

There may be an ego satisfaction when we take on a job that somebody is having a tough time with; but if it messes up our schedule of work or gets us overloaded in general then we may have to forego some of the ego reward by saying no.

Another cause of our attempting too much is that we're overly ambitious. This may be a part of the ego problem we just mentioned or it may be that we don't have a very realistic view of what we can do and can't do in the time allotted. Whatever the case, we need to realize that most projects take longer than we first think they will because of interferences that distract our attention and because of things that others fail to do for us in the project. If we're going to continue to improve our ability to perform up to our ambition level, we must get our time estimates properly established.

There is nothing wrong with being ambitious, the problem is that if our ambition allows us to take on so much work that we either fail to do the job well, or don't have time to learn from the jobs we are doing then our ambition is getting in our way rather than helping us.

Let's looks at another case of poor time management – being disorganized. No matter what we may think, we can't work effectively in the midst of confusion with things piled up on our desk, stuff on the floor, files poorly kept on our computer, or anything else that makes our workspace look like a landfill site. There are those who argue that since they work on more than one project at a time, they have to have more than one thing on their desk at a time.

Chapter 6

This may be true, but those who are organized at least have several things in some kind of order. The argument that, "I can find anything on the desk I need without any trouble," doesn't work, because the fact that we feel the need to defend the shape of our work space proves that it is more disorganized than it ought to be.

Even if we are working on several projects and find anything in a pile of confusion, we need some place to work that isn't confusing or distracting. The appearance of things out of place and disorganized isn't very healthy and won't help our thought processes very much. So, how can we get rid of this problem of poor organization? Let's look at some of the answers.

First: never let more than one pile of material accumulate on our desk at one time. This doesn't mean that we let the pile get higher and higher. If we find that we need two or three stacks of things on or around our work area, we know that we're taking on too much or not finishing enough. We should take some time to finish some of the projects before we take on more. We may be having a problem with procrastination, getting something almost finished and taking on something else before we take the last steps on the first job.

Another cause of personal disorganization is the matter of just not filing things very well on our computer. We may not know how to maximize electronic files and folders or have a poor system. Whatever the reason, having a place for something, putting it there and being able to find it when we need it, is the best solution. A good e-filing system is key and simplicity is best. As soon as we decide that something needs to be filed, we need to

Chapter 6

decide where it should be filed and ensure that it gets put there. There is no reason for it to stay on our desk or in our inbox after we've decided that we are done with this for now. We have to learn to delete files that are no longer needed, so our files do not become too large or too difficult to work with. A good rule to follow on files is to set a time limit like two or three years then go through and find all those things we haven't accessed in that period of time. Unless there is some legal requirement to keep these things, or unless we have proof that we will need them shortly, delete them. The time we will save by not having to hunt through unorganized files will offset the occasional absence of things we'd like to use that have been deleted.

One good way to get and stay organized is to just let our day happen. There's a thing called 'overcoat' syndrome that describes how many people start their day. They come in with their coat on, the phone rings, someone down the hall needs to meet with them, someone is waiting for them in their office and whatever some person asks for is what gets the day started.

To start each day in this manner means that we will never be in control of our work lives; others get control before we even get our coats off. The solution to this problem is much simpler than we think, it just takes a little planning. The night before, we make a list of things that we want to accomplish; that way, we have the next day set up for a much smoother and organized operation. Then, when we meet the person in the hall or the phone rings as we come in the door, we can say, "I'll be glad to get on that as soon as I can. I have to do this first..." We should never feel badly about telling people we are busy, that we have a

Chapter 6

planned program of work, or that we are working things that are important.

External Time Wasters

So far we've looked at time wasters that we some control over, such things as attempting too much and poor personal organization. Now, let's think about things that we have less control over – "external" causes. The most obvious one is that unscheduled interruption that comes by phone, an email, a text or in the form of a drop-in visitor with nothing else to do but talk. Of course, not all unscheduled interruptions come from people who are just passing the time. They may have legitimate reasons for wanting to see us or communicate with us. It's just that their interruptions can't be scheduled and therefore disrupt our planned day. Let's look at these problems and see what we can do to get a little control over our lives, even when the problem is caused by someone else.

First, there is the matter of the *drop-in visitor*. We're working on something that we've scheduled that has a tight time line and along comes someone who decides to treat us with a visit. It may be a friend who just wants to visit; it may be someone looking for a place to hide from work; it may be someone who has a legitimate reason to see us but didn't have the courtesy to call ahead to let us know they were coming; it may even be the boss who may or may not have a good reason for interrupting us. Whoever it is and for whatever reason, they're in our office. What do we do?

Chapter 6

Before we look at some solutions to the problem of what to do after they get there, let's see if there's something we can do to prevent them from being there in the first place. We need to see if there is something about our workplace that is particularly inviting to people looking for a place to "visit." We may have our work station turned toward the door in such a way that everyone can see in and see a vacant chair, which may be a temptation to drop in.

We may be sitting in such a way that we look right at people as if we are inviting them in. Even if we aren't in an open-invitation mode, there may be something about our behavior that keeps people coming back. Maybe we're *too* friendly. Maybe in our effort not to hurt anyone's feelings, we've created the idea that we don't have to much to do and welcome visitors.

We may be so helpful when they're with us that we cause them to come back for more help. It's not that we don't want to be helpful and that we don't want to do our job, but we should be helpful only in those things that pertain to our job. If someone has come in and wanted something that we don't usually do, and we've gone out of our way to find an answer for them, we've actually encouraged them to come back. We must remember that when people are looking for help to get their job done, they aren't particular about who helps them.

Even if it isn't our job to do it, they will keep coming back as long as they get the help they need. It may be time for us to direct them to the right person or place so they will stop coming back.

Chapter 6

We have to admit that most of us enjoy a certain amount of socializing, so if we have done it in the past, we can't expect people to stop coming to see us just because we've decided to get busy for a change. But if we've come to the conclusion that these visits are costing us valuable time, we need to start somewhere. We start by being busy, letting people know we're busy and doing things in a business like manner.

We will have to give the impression that we're doing something important, something we've planned to do and that we *are busy*. That's the rule for dealing with *anyone*, including the boss who drops in to see us unannounced. Let visitors know we're busy, that we're doing something important and that we are on a schedule. This doesn't mean that we don't also give the impression that we want to help, but the offer to help comes *after* we've established these other ideas. When they say, "How's it going?" we answer by saying, "Fine. I'm just trying to get this project out by eleven o'clock. What can I do for you?" It's that simple.

Suppose the visitor doesn't leave even after we've established our work schedule? Then we don't have to worry as much about hurting their feelings. We don't have to be rude. If, after we've explained our work load, visitors don't catch on that we don't have time to socialize, then they aren't so sensitive that they're likely to get their feelings hurt too quickly. We may have to get up and move towards the door. It is hard for them to stay seated when we stand. When they get up, we simply say, "It's good to see you...let's have lunch one day soon." With some people we may do well not to sit down at all. When they come in, we meet them at the door and block the way while we talk to them, make small conversation, establish our busy schedule and then politely bid them farewell. The problem with all of this is that it sounds like we're playing games – and really we are. By far the best thing we can do is come right out and tell them we are busy, can't talk right now and will try to get back to them later. The reason we don't do this is that we worry about hurting people's feeling, or we're embarrassed to be that bold, or we're afraid of how they will react.

To some extent, these are all good reasons, but they lead us to playing games. We must decide whether we want to play games or learn how to be more direct.

The unexpected call, email, or text is one of the greatest time wasters.

Let's talk about another time waster that's external in nature – the unexpected call, email, or text. These things are perhaps the greatest time wasters that are the easiest to overlook. It may not take long to respond to these things but throughout the day the time can really add up and distract you from what you were working on.

The important thing to remember about these interruptions is that they are most impolite event in our day. Even the most rude and insensitive person would not come into your office when we are talking to someone, physically come between us and start talking, expecting the other person to have no feelings about the interruption. Every time we respond to a call, email or text, we've allowed the sender to do just that. We need to

Chapter 6

establish strong habits to deal with these types of interruptions.

The rule for this is the same as for the drop-in visitor; establish that we're busy doing something important on a planned schedule. We establish this early and then let the caller go from there. If he or she doesn't choose to respect our time, at least we have made it clear that we have other things to do, which gives us a reason to end the communication if we need to. If it's a phone call, we establish our schedule by making that the first thing we say in the conversation.

When the person says, "Hello, how's it going?" we answer with our busy-important-scheduled answer. "Not bad... just trying to get some things done for our production department before lunch. What can I do for you?" As we've said before, now it's up to them to decide if they have something more important to talk about.

If we have somebody in our office that we are *not trying* to get rid of, we say, "Just having a meeting with Steve about the overtime schedule, we should be done soon, is there something I can do quickly for you or would you like me to call you back when I have more time?" The politeness is there and we've made it clear that we want to help; but we've gotten the message across that we've got something important going on.

In all we've said about time management, we've tried to say that our goal is to let others know we're busy and that we're doing something important on a schedule. This will save us time only if we actually are busy *and* if we do spend our time on important things *and* if we do plan

Chapter 6

some kind of workable schedule. It's not enough to get more time and protect the time we have. *We have to use the time well when we get it.* This means we need a plan, we need to follow that plan and we need to check at the end of the day to see if we accomplished what we set out to do. We also need to ask if we are doing what we ought to be doing, or if someone else should be doing this. We'll talk more about delegation in another chapter. For now we'll say that more people waste valuable time doing what others should be doing, than doing their own things properly.

Organizing

So far we've talked about only a part of what is necessary to set up the work. There is another function called organizing that plays a big parting getting us to the final objective we have set. Organizing is a pretty broad term and generally includes two things: the *structure* of the organization we have set up to do the job and the *people* in the organization.

Since higher management usually handles the structure of the organization, we'll look mostly at the part concerning people. Note that we aren't talking about something big and complicated when we use the word "organization." We're simply talking about any group of people who have joined together to get something done that they couldn't do themselves. This fits the small work group in one location as well as it does an entire organization of thousands of people across many states or countries – and the same principles apply.

Chapter 6

Since part of organizing includes staffing the organization, we should realize that when it comes time to fill a vacancy in our group we will be expected to do an interview. Since the prospective employee will be working in our organization, we should look forward to meeting and finding out as much as possible about him or her.

Most new managers dread this aspect of the job. With a little knowledge of how to conduct the interview and a little experience, these fears will diminish considerably. We will talk in detail about the interview process in an upcoming chapter.

Right Person – Right Job

The whole purpose of the staffing phase of organizing is to try to match up the potential of the employee with the requirements of the job. Unfortunately, we often find that through poor staffing we end up making ourselves and our employees suffer. Often we do a poor job of matching an employee's skills and interests with the job then blame the employee for poor performance. We should really blame ourselves for poor judgment.

Getting the right people to do the right job makes a lot of sense from a lot of standpoints. Obviously, employees who are doing the jobs for which they are well suited have fewer frustrations, they see that they are useful to the organization and feel that they have a chance to be recognized. As a result, they are most likely to be motivated to do their best and will probably be satisfied employees.

Chapter 6

From our standpoint as the manager, a lot of our problems are solved because the employee's motivation should help reduce absenteeism and turnover and increase productivity. We will then have more time to handle other phases of our job. From the organization's standpoint, it is not only getting value for wages paid – it is also getting a good picture of *us* in the process.

When our people perform well, it naturally reflects *favorably* on us. Note, too, that a mismatch between employees and job can also make all of these things come out *unfavorable*.

There is another phase of organizing which we will in detail in a later chapter; that is *training*. It isn't enough to try to get employees and their jobs matched as well as possible. We must still make up the difference between the employee's present skills and the job requirements.

This can be best done by training. Given enough time and patience, the employees may in fact learn on their own, but this is rarely the most efficient way or the most practical approach from the organization's standpoint. Not only do we need to have the employees know their job, *we need to know* that they know how to do their work.

Training gives us this knowledge, because we see that they have had an opportunity to learn the skill. If it's good training, we will see them actually demonstrating their proficiency. Then if they do not do their job properly, we look for another cause other than lack of training.

Chapter 6

Review

We have often defined the manager's job as getting the job done through other people. However, a portion of the manager's job includes some other functions. They have many different names but we'll classify them into four functions: planning, organizing, directing and controlling. Two of these, planning and organizing, have to do with setting the work up, the other two have to do with getting the work done. The world is full of proverbs about having a goal, but the one that best describes it, is: "If you don't know where you are going any road will get you there." Many organizations never get anywhere because they don't really know where they want to go. Managers should always think in terms of planning, planning and planning. As simple as that sounds, it isn't easy to do with all of the other things that are going on around you. Once have decided what to do, it's equally important to see that the right people are doing it. This comes under the function of the organizing. It's not enough just to plan: we must act on that plan. In simple terms, it's a matter of the right people doing the right things at the right time. Any time the manager has control over this function, it's important that attention be paid to it, rather than just let things be done as they always have. When we do it this way and neglect our responsibility, we give rise to the old saying, "There's no special reason for doing it this way; we've just always done it this way."

Chapter 7

Getting the Work Done - Directing and Controlling

Planning and organizing – set the stage for the next two functions: *directing* and *controlling*. The best of plans and the best organizations won't do the work. Only those under us can do it and we must direct them in doing it and control their efforts while doing it. Planning and organizing are done at higher levels in the organization, while directing and controlling are done at the lower levels. As new managers, we must be very aware of the functions of directing and controlling.

Directing

Directing involves people and people can be complicated. We often disagree with one another, our views can change constantly, our needs and emotions can change, making us unpredictable. As managers, we need to understand that many people can react differently under different circumstances.

Chapter 7

However, there are some common areas in which people will react the same way all the time. There are things we can do that will give us predictable results, even though we do them to people who are very different one another. Once we have learned these things, we can build our 'management philosophy' around them.

There are 3 areas of directing: leading, communicating, and motivating.

Leading: If you ask a dozen people what leadership means, you will probably get a dozen different answers. A good definition of leadership is *the ability of a manager to inspire their workers to work hard to achieve the goals of the organization.* We know that good leaders are made – not born, and all of us can be better than we are. There are things that we can learn that will produce better results. There are skills of leadership that can be practiced, learned and measured. There are some characteristics that are shared by people who have had great success and we can develop these as we get more experience and training.

Successful leaders usually have the ability to see other people's point of view. They don't necessarily agree with them or give in to them, but they at least have some empathy for those positions. They are sensitive to other people's problems and know why people feel the way they do. Successful leaders know how what they say will be taken and how it will affect other people. They probably know how those individuals will react to certain things that are done and if the reaction is different from what they expect, they may even be able to analyze why it's different.

Self-awareness is the ability to see how what we say or do will influence others.

Another characteristic good leaders have is the ability to see themselves as others see them. Self-awareness is the ability to see how what we say or do will influence others. We should know how what we say will sound from the point of view of others. Will they resent it, miss the point or agree with it in principle? Good leaders can predict the answer pretty closely. Good leaders will even know their own weaknesses and faults and try to build around them. They don't let such flaws interfere with either their own performance or that of others. The important thing about seeing ourselves as others see us is that we are more likely to treat others fairly if we know that they are reacting to something that we have said or done and especially if we know *why* they are reacting that way.

Another characteristic of successful leaders that we can all learn is the willingness to work. There are few substitutes for hard work and for leaders there are none. The type of work that leaders do is different from that done by those who are not leaders. Leaders are willing to put in long hours on tasks that are not exciting or

Chapter 7

rewarding and quite possibly unpleasant – *just get the job done*. This doesn't mean that they don't know how to delegate; it means that they don't avoid the tasks that have to be done sooner or later.

When they see that a particular task has to be done and it's their job to do it, they tackle it without thinking about getting out of it or putting it off until later. Of all the characteristics of a successful leader, this may be the most difficult of them all.

Still another common characteristic of successful leaders is their ability to generate enthusiasm among their people. This will project itself from the leaders and catches on with their people. This ability to generate enthusiasm comes out differently in different leaders, but the results are the same. Their workers tackle their jobs with interest and excitement and will get satisfaction from their work.

A final common characteristic among good leaders is the willingness to accept responsibility. Good leaders become very bored when there is little or no responsibility connected with what they are doing. They aren't afraid to accept the challenge of doing something that has risk to it. They are willing to take on a job that may allow them to fail, providing it allows them the opportunity to succeed. They may even go out and look for responsibility if they don't get it otherwise. Instead of waiting for someone to give them authority to do something, they will probably be pushing the top of the responsibility ladder. If they get called into question, it will be for talking on too much responsibility, not too little.

Chapter 7

Communicating: When we can get a specific message across to another person or a group *in just the way we want it to get across*, that's good communication. Whether we are writing emails, speaking to groups or individuals, giving direction or conveying policies, we haven't ended our responsibilities until the message is *received and understood*.

The best measure of our ability to communicate is to see whether what we said produced the results we were trying to get. The best sign that our message has gotten through successfully is to see if the policy is being carried out, people are coming in on time, or if they are responding in a way that indicates that they really understood the message sent.

One final word about good communicating – *it is not just an asset, but a requirement of the job*. Managers must accept the responsibility for what they communicate. They cannot blame the subordinates for not getting the message; the manager must ensure the message is clear, even if it means doing the communicating all over again. They must also work as hard to communicate up the line as down. Their own bosses and bosses up the line must manage as well as they can on the basis of the information they receive from below.

Motivating: Motivation is a little different from leadership in that leadership inspires people to work for external reasons – often for the leader – while motivation gets them to work for internal reasons – because they want to, regardless of how they may feel about the organization. Motivation is probably the single most important aspect of the manager's job. We can't *make* the

Chapter 7

employees work for very long and expect a good job from them. The desire to work must come from within the individual if it's going to last.

But now we have a problem, because it's the specific responsibility of the manager to see that the workers feel this way about their job and that they *want* to work. This means that we can't just say, "Well it's not my fault, they just don't want to work." When we say that, we are openly admitting that we are doing a bad job of managing. This doesn't mean that we won't run into this problem, it just means that we have to accept the responsibility of correcting it.

In order to motivate our people, we have to understand why people work in the first place and what it is that makes them work harder or keeps them from working as hard as they can. Of course, the basic needs are for food, clothing, shelter and safety. But once these needs have been satisfied, people still have certain social needs that must be met and they are motivated when they see a chance to meet these needs. For instance, they want to be accepted by their fellow workers. They want to think that they are liked and that others want to have them around. They want to be an accepted part of the work group.

Managers must recognize this and make every effort to help the workers feel that they are an important part of the organization and that the other workers respect their work. We can do this by reflecting any favorable remarks we hear. "By the way, Steven really liked that you were put in charge of this project..." Very few managers have become successful by sowing discord and suspicion among their workers.

Chapter 7

Another need the workers have is for self-esteem. This is related to what we just said, in that people like to think that the job they are doing is important and that they are good at it. It's hard for any of us to get motivated over a job that has been downgraded and specified as not really that important in the organization. That's why people worry about job titles, name plates or being on the official company website. They like people to know that they are important enough to the organization to be recognized. Such little things will often go a long way to meeting these needs. But employees want to feel that the other employees respect them for their ability to do the job.

Correct in private and approve in public.

They want others to think that what they do is important and they like to think that others look up to them for their ability. But when we come along and criticize an employee in front of the other employees, we not only put that employee in an embarrassing position, we also destroy the self esteem that is so important to them. That's the main reason why we are always told to *correct in private and approve in public*.

In discussing these three points – leading, communicating and motivating, it is just common sense to recognize that certain things will cause workers to work better and that we should take advantage of these things. This is a calculated effort to get the best results from the individuals who work for us. We expect our employees to give their equipment the proper care and maintenance; how could we possibly do less for them? It is our way of getting employees to work because they *want* to, not because the *have* to. In the end, the results are better for the organization, for the manager and definitely for the employees.

Controlling

While directing is often the most difficult function, controlling is perhaps the most *critical*. When we plan, organize and direct, there is still the problem of controlling all of what we have planned, organized and are directing. Without proper controls, all the effort may be wasted. Essentially, managers control three things of a combination of them – *money, material and people*. The problem is that each is handled differently and each takes a different skill.

We find it is easier to budget money and materials because they are usually quite constant. But people aren't that easy to budget; they aren't all alike and even a single individual may show different qualities on different days. While a dollar is a dollar, a worker isn't a worker. Replace one admin staff with another and the results can be quite different. When we start to budget (control) people, we have to consider that they may work at different speeds in the morning than in the afternoon; their attitudes and behavior may be different on a Friday than on a Monday.

Controlling is most closely related to planning, which simply says that we must have something to control. Often we may find ourselves trying to control when we actually haven't got a plan to follow. The plan serves as

Chapter 7

the *standard* against which we control, so without the plan we are doing guesswork with our controlling.

For example, when we decide in the middle of a project that the costs are too high and we start to *control*, we really aren't measuring this against our preset standard (or plan), so it isn't completely correct to say we are practicing the function of control. If we had planned correctly and started our controlling as soon as the plan went into effect, things wouldn't have gotten out of hand in the first place. When we find ourselves in a drastic situation with people, materials or money, either the planning or the controlling stage has broken down at some point.

Steps in Controlling

We generally think of controlling as consisting of three steps:

> Determining standards
> Measuring results against standards
> Taking remedial action as required

As we have said, the plan is the standard, but now we are looking for the answer to certain basic questions. We need to know who sets the standards and how will we know that they are the standards. The plan may or may not have specified how far off the standards we can get without being in trouble. That is information we must have; we cannot control without it. Another thing we need to know about the standards is who will measure the results of our work and who will see the results of those

Chapter 7

measurements. Is there a quality control person who reports to our head office or do we have someone internally that has partial responsibility for approving quality?

The most important question is – *what will be measured*? Why is this particular thing being measured? We will obviously want to measure the output of goods or services and ask – How long did it take to provide the service or turn out the product? How much money did it take? What was the final quality and how many did we actually produce? Then we need to closely look at the expenses.

When we measure expenses, we must measure *all* of them. Are we taking into account everything that is being charged to a particular project? Are considering staff help, hidden costs, load factors and other costs that will eventually have to be accounted for?

Another thing that we must account for is the use of resources. Again we are talking about people, time and money – but this time in a different light. Here the question of measurement is one of *efficient use*. Are we doing a good job of matching people to the job?

Remember it isn't necessarily proof of good management if the job gets done well. We must consider who's doing the job. If our people are capable of doing much more because of experience, education or talent, we can't be too proud of the fact that the job is done well. The key is to match ability and job requirements as closely as possible then let the people grow out of their jobs as they develop.

Chapter 7

As managers we must constantly measure how well the employee is matched to the job or whether they have outgrown it.

All of this is true for the other resources we have. Are we really getting the most out of our overtime? Are we doing some jobs that could be left undone or eliminated altogether, then using time and money on overtime to do essential things?

We get trapped sometimes by saying that we have to go into overtime to do a very important job, failing to realize that we got into this situation simply because we failed to control our time properly. We spent valuable time on unimportant things, forcing ourselves into overtime. The same objection applies to using people on nonessential details when they could be doing things that must be done sooner or later. It's all right for everyone to pitch in and help, but if this pitching in means that we must neglect other work that will get us behind schedule or cost us time or money later on, then we've made a bad decision.

Using the Budget to Control

Perhaps the oldest and best control device we have is the budget. We complain about it and even wish we didn't have it, but we should be glad that there is something as rigid as the budget to guide us in our controlling. Very few organizations could run smoothly without a budget because it gives us one of the best standards we could ask for. As we constantly compare ourselves with the budget, we are also getting feedback on where we can expect to end up at the end of the budget period. This is a means of measuring even the smallest part of the job, because budgets are made up of parts.

Good budgets are made up of *accurate* parts and bad budgets are made up of *padded* parts. Budgets are put together to let the organization know how much money there is and where the best places to spend it are. Good budget planning takes into account local needs and those putting it together will solicit help from all levels in determining the best use of all the money. The trouble comes when each level starts to be unrealistic about their needs. When each group or division adds just a little, by the time the total budget is drawn up, there is either too big a demand or the organization finds itself looking for more money than it really needs. When this happens, the fate of most budgets is that someone at the top starts to carve it down and everyone gets hurt. We shouldn't include anything we can't substantiate, because sooner or later we will have to account for what we have asked for. If our figures don't stand the test, not only will our budget be cut, but our reputation as a manager will suffer. The wisest thing to do is to make a realistic budget, back it up with a good set of requirements, then let upper management wrestle with the problem of cutting it if they have to. Later on, if the work isn't done because of budget problems, we can show that we put in a legitimate request that got cut by someone else.

Measuring Results

Once we have determined the standards by which we are to control, we have to measure the results *against these standards*. Sometimes this measurement is routine – just a matter of how many units were produced, how many

Chapter 7

pages were formatted, how many sales were made, then reporting the obvious results in whatever manner is provided. But not all of our evaluating is that obvious or that easy. Sometimes we find ourselves in situations in which there are so many contributing factors that we aren't quite sure just what the results mean. It may be that the operation is too large, like a large assembly line with many feed-ins, or that there are many people making different contributions to the end product – or the output may be service and that means there is the customer to consider. How can we measure in situations like this?

One of the best processes available to us is known as *sampling*. There isn't anything complicated about it. It's just a means of looking at large or complicated operations and getting reliable results without having to get a measurement on every detail and every person doing work on the project.

We simply look at a small, average sample and take the results to represent the entire operation. We can do a pretty good job of sampling and get very reliable results. Once we get in the habit of doing this, we are on the lookout for ways of getting true samples all of the time. We check the absentee list on random occasions and see if particular individuals or a particular number are absent.

We spot check three or four days in a row and see just how much time our workers are taking for break or when they are coming in from lunch. We look at customer complaints once a week for several weeks and see if there is any one thing starting to give us trouble.

Chapter 7

These things are good indicators of just how well we are doing and good means of controlling.

When sampling doesn't seem to be a very good way of measuring the results and the measuring seems to be too difficult on the whole operation, there is another way that may help. This is a matter of finding a *substitute* measurement. For example, we can look at such things as absenteeism and get a good idea of what the morale is within the group. If the turnover is high, this may be a good substitute measurement of how much job enrichment is going on.

A look at previous production records may be a good measure of how much motivation or employee morale exists in the group, providing other things are equal. The substitute may be a tangible means of measuring very intangible things such as attitudes, job satisfaction, morale, etc.

When we are measuring one thing to look at something else, we had better be sure the measure is accurate, which is true of any of our measurements. Even measuring such things as how well a sales rep is doing compared to others in the country may not give true results. We need to be careful in evaluating one sales rep's results against another's until we are sure the territories are the same. It's all right to measure sales as a means of determining the success of a sales rep, providing we know what other sales reps in the same or similar territories have done. If a sales rep isn't doing as well as they should be, what is the potential in that territory? Is the competition getting stronger? Does the sales rep really know the new products? Have they had the proper training and the

Chapter 7

same training as the other sales reps? Can we ensure our measurement is really accurate in all respects? If so, then it becomes a good control device; if not, it becomes a dangerous tool to use in making decisions.

Remedial Action

Controlling would be useless if it didn't include the final action of control – taking remedial action when it is required. When things are shown by our measuring processes to be running smoothly then we should be good enough managers to recognize this and leave things alone. But when the results show that the situation is getting out of control or that we really should be doing better, then we need to know enough to step in and take appropriate action. We may not be the ones to take the action, but we may be the ones to instigate it.

As obvious as this seems, just knowing that something is wrong isn't enough; reporting it to the right people is important. If we have found that a problem exists somewhere in the group, we should ask ourselves: who really needs to know about this? The answer should be: someone who can do something about it. Whether it's an overtime problem or a union grievance, telling the right person as soon as possible may head off a much more serious problem later on.

It's our problem as soon as we hear or know about it, and it's our problem until something is done about it or someone else takes over responsibility for the problem. When our boss says, "Ok, I'll take over now," then we have done all we can, even if we don't like what they decide to do.

Chapter 7

Another important point of notifying the right person at the right time is to do it the right way. If the person doesn't get the importance of the problem or misses some of the details, we've got to accept the responsibility for the poor results that come from improper control.

The best approach is to put the problem in writing (email) which not only puts the information in permanent form but also provides a record that we spotted the weakness and made an effort to get it controlled.

It is always better to solve the problem ourselves than to pass it along to others. This means we must have the authority to take necessary remedial action. It also means that we may have to go over the entire planning, organizing and directing functions all over again. If that's what he remedial action requires, being a good manager means doing it that way, rather than just closing our eyes to reality and going ahead toward eventual poor results.

Discipline

Part of getting the work done through others and part of directing others, is using properly administered discipline to correct behavior or to prevent poor performance. Discipline can be unpleasant and it is something that neither the manager nor employee looks forward to. But when it is necessary, it should be done properly. There are some rules to follow for successful discipline.

Rule #1: Be Consistent. Nothing is completely fair in this world, but some things don't need as much *fairness*

Chapter 7

as others. When we are handing out praise and give somebody too much, he or she rarely complains about the unfairness. But when we hand out an seemingly unfair amount of discipline, people resent it and are quick to let us know about it. This means we must strive to maintain some kind of consistency in the things we do. If one person gets suspended for being late four times in a month, anybody and everybody should be suspended for being late four times in a month. The consistency must hold for our own employees and other employees in other departments. It will quickly undermine our efforts if someone in another department hands out a different type of punishment for the same infraction and we can undermine other managers if we don't strive to keep our own efforts in line with theirs.

Rule #2: Avoid Emotions. If we must offer some form of punishment to an employee who performs unsatisfactorily, we must avoid getting emotionally involved when we discuss the situation with the employee. If we see that the employee has made us angry or if we are exasperated with their behavior, then we'll be better off to postpone the action until we have had a chance to cool off. Even if the employee loses his or her cool and gets childish about the matter, we must still have the dignity and patience to do the right thing.

Rule #3: Match Crime with Punishment. It is a serious thing to invoke the power of the job to discipline someone. When one person has the power to make another person lose pay, miss days of work or have poor ratings added to a personnel record, it is not be taken lightly. In any society it is necessary that there be order; this means that someone must have higher accountability

Chapter 7

than others and therefore, the right to exercise control. If this control means that we must discipline someone, we want the discipline to match the person's misbehavior as much as possible. Not only are we consistent this way, but we are also striving to be fair in the process.

Rule #4: Discipline for Improved Performance. The problem with calling any form of discipline 'punishment' is that it tends to make us look backward instead of forward. If we look back, we see only poor performance and we see the punishment as a way to get even with the employee for this misconduct. If we look ahead, we see the punishment as a means to correct the behavior and thus provide us with good performance in the future. Discipline serves two basic functions: 1. It keeps the employee from repeating the poor performance. 2. It tends to keep others from committing the same violation of the workplace rules.

Rule #5: Provide an "Out" for Good Behavior. One problem we have in exercising a firm hand is that we fail to have provisions for employees to "clean" their records. When an employee violates the organization's rules to such extent that some form of discipline must be administered, this goes on the employee's record. We also have to find a way to put something in the records when poor performance is corrected. If we use a 'demerit' system, we need to have a counterpart in a 'merit' system.

Rule #6: Don't Delay Discipline. Even though we've said that we don't want to discipline when we're emotionally involved with the situation, we don't want to delay action so long that the employee will lose the significance of the event and the action we're taking. If we are trying to ensure that the poor performance doesn't repeat itself, the action we take should be as closely related to that poor performance as we can make it.

Rule #7: Don't Hold Grudges. When an employee does something wrong, remember that it is the performance we don't like, not the individual. If we make the mistake of holding the action against the person, then we're starting to get vindictive.

Obviously there are more rules than these seven, but these will go a long way toward making us good disciplinarians. One of the first things we must establish is; does the employee know the standard on which his or her performance is based? This means we must ask ourselves, "Is there a standard?" If the answer is no, then we don't have to go any further; we can't discipline if there is no standard to go by. The standards need to be realistic, measurable, and doable.

Next, we ask ourselves, "Does the employee know the standard?" If we haven't explained our expectations with the employee and how we will measure performance, we can't go any further. We can't hand out discipline to an employee who doesn't know what to expect. We might expand this question to include, "Has the employee been trained to meet the standard?" It is not enough that we have a standard and we've told the employee what we expect. If we haven't trained the employees how to do what we want them to do and haven't seen them do it correctly, we aren't on very safe ground when the times comes to discipline them.

Chapter 7

The next question we ask is, "Have we told the employee how we feel about his or her performance?" Many managers will talk about their employees, but not *to* them. We'll tell other managers about the bad performance we are getting, but we never call the employee in to discuss the behavior. This is a very personal thing. We start off by saying "Here's how I see your performance." Then we offer documentation, specific occasions when these things happened, or when things either weren't done properly or not at all. We compare this to the standard and show why we feel the employee has under performed. If we haven't been open and honest with the employee and don't have documentation, we aren't ready for discipline.

We then ask ourselves, "Does the employee know the consequences for continued poor performance?" Most organizations practice 'progressive discipline', meaning that for each offense the discipline gets more and more severe, possibly leading to dismissal. If we haven't explained this to the employee, we can't really go further with disciplinary steps. In addition, the employee should also know the consequences for improved performance.

Now we ask, "Has a date been set for a review of the employee's performance?" Many good managers find this to be their downfall. They do everything right up to this point, then say "I want to see you straighten this out as soon as possible" without setting a deadline for review. The review should be as soon as the employee has had a chance to perform the task a sufficient number of times, or as soon as there is chance to show that the correction has been made. If the employee has been late several times in a month, we should set a time for review in a

Chapter 7

month or 6 weeks, giving the employee time to make corrections in his or her personal life.

As we've said, discipline isn't easy, but by following these rules and asking these questions, we'll be on much safer ground, especially if we remember one important thing: *whenever we discipline, we must always have specific documentation for the things we are talking about.* This means dates, times, amounts and situations. We won't get very far if we go in and say, "I'm going to have to discipline you because you are late all the time..."

Documentation

We've spent some time talking about discipline, but we don't want it to sound like all of our emphasis should be on disciplining employees. Our goal is always to get the most out of our employees with the least effort on our part. The ideal is that all employees will perform to a high level, will be interested in their jobs and will try to excel. We would hope that each person is looking for a way to improve his or her performance. We are always looking for employees who need little or no correction or only an occasional training or coaching session. These are the things that we aim for, but only get occasionally or perhaps never, from all of our employees at the same time. Therefore, we will need to do some correction or discipline, but the steps we've just discussed should help us do the job more easily.

There is another phase of watching performance that we need to give attention to. Like discipline, it sounds like we're watching the employees too closely and may give the perception that we don't trust them. That's not the

Chapter 7

case. It is the matter of *documentation*. It is embarrassing when we confront an employee for some infraction and they discover that we don't have accurate records of when and where the infraction took place. When we say to employees, "You've been late a lot recently," and don't have the dates and times, it sounds pretty weak. If we say, "You're always negative about your assignments," without any specific information, we are going to lose any argument that comes up. This means that we keep dates, times, instances, situations, quotations, etc. so we can come back and document our discussion if we need to. Good managers make a habit of keeping records though they may not expect or plan to use the information. The rule to remember is that 'documentation after the fact' doesn't hold much water. Simply trying to remember the days the employee got into an argument with another person on the same shift, or failed to report a piece of equipment that working improperly, or came in 20 minutes late, isn't likely to give us good information to use when we have to confront the employee in a discipline situation. Remember we aren't spying: we're simply keeping track of facts and situations as they happen.

Review

There two parts to planning: planning the work and working the plan. We can't say which one is more important. We can only say that unless each is done well, the results will suffer drastically. We've seen that getting the work done takes both directing and controlling. We have to emphasize that directing people is neither leading

Chapter 7

nor pushing: *we're pointing the way*. Since our job as managers is to see that others do the work, we demonstrate our best directing not by our visibility or screaming orders from the throne, but by motivating, encouraging and helping others do the work *because they want to*.

The successful managers are the ones who direct by getting the people to believe in the job, not the boss. It's all right to believe in the boss, but that alone shouldn't be the reason they work. If we are really going to be a success at managing, we have to give up the idea that only *born leaders* make good managers. We have to understand that management is simply a long list of well done skills, each of which can be learned. Directing people is one of those important skills.

Controlling is the least exciting and perhaps the most critical of the skills required in getting the job done. It's a matter of knowing what's going on and knowing it soon enough to do something about it before it's too late to correct the direction things are taking. It takes attention to details. It takes looking at records. It means knowing for sure what we expect and seeing how close we come to those expectations. It means that we have to have a certain amount of flexibility and agility to move fast to correct a bad situation. It's the last chance we have to correct poor planning and poor directing. If we're good enough at it, we can turn even a bad situation into one that gets the job done on schedule.

Chapter 8

Motivating by Enriching the Job

Motivation has long been a subject of discussion among managers and those who provide management training. Obviously we want out people to be motivated. If they are, then they will work harder, be more pleasant and enjoy their jobs more – with the result that they get the work done and make our job easier. A worthy goal, but one that puts a lot of responsibility on motivation and becomes difficult to reach if we aren't sure how to motivate our people.

Why Do People Work?

In order to understand how to motivate people on the job, it's necessary to find out why people work in the first place. But the question goes deeper than that because what we really want to know is what gives people the

Chapter 8

most satisfaction. If we find this out, then we know what makes them work and even what will make them work harder.

Those who have studied the matter in great detail have found out some interesting things about why people work. At first it would seem that everyone works to make money. People do expect to get paid, they enjoy the things that money can bring and they would like to make more money. But they don't work just for money.

Primarily, people do what they do to meet certain needs or to get satisfactions. People worry about their families' security, so they work to care of this need. Food, clothing and shelter are concerns for any worker, so these are strong motivating factors. People also like to be liked. They like to have loved ones who care about them, but this need is met outside the job.

A Higher Need

But most of us have other needs that can be met on the job. In fact, they must be met before the employee is truly motivated. We all like to have our egos 'uplifted'. We like to think we are useful. We like to contribute something for which we get the credit. This is a need that comes to the surface frequently in all of us and is the one factor that a manager can always depend on for use in motivation.

For a long time managers tried to motivate their people by making the work location a pleasant place. Often better lighting was installed, along with effective heat and air conditioning. Managers were often trained in human

Chapter 8

relations so they would know exactly how to handle the employees that worked for them. In addition to the standard benefits some companies developed other benefits like tuition for employees who wanted to go to school and scholarships for the employee's families. Surely with all of these benefits, in addition to attractive wages and vacation plans, the employees were motivated almost of out of control – *but they weren't.* There is an interesting thing about the benefits mentioned above. If the workers in one area have them, those who don't will be dissatisfied, perhaps even lack motivation. But the presence of such benefits seldom produces motivation over a prolonged period. There is no evidence to show that day in and day out, employees work harder because of a good health benefit plan. Even when employees get an increase in wages, it rarely motivates them on a permanent basis. So do we remove all these things because they don't motivate the employees? Obviously not, because their absence will do more harm even if the benefits don't serve to motivate them.

The Key to Motivation

If none of these things motivate people to work hard over a long period of time, what's left for the manager to do? Actually the answer is simple, although carrying it out is pretty hard. *The job itself* holds the key to motivation. The job is the one thing that can provide employees with the satisfaction they need to be motivated. They want a chance to succeed; they want recognition; they want to feel that they have a chance to advance; the want to feel that they are making a contribution to the organization. All the benefit plans in the world will not provide these satisfactions. Only the work can do it.

Chapter 8

But there is potential danger here. *The job can also prevent these needs from being met.* The new manager may fall into the trap that many older ones are in now. We may fail to use the job as the best means of motivating our workers. In fact, when we take over our assignment from the last manager who had it, we may find that the motivating factors have been removed. If we just go along doing what the last manager did, we may miss a great opportunity to provide motivation, get more work done and look good in the process. Now let's see how this works.

Remember, we are looking for ways in which the employees' desire for recognition, achievement and chance for advancement can be satisfied right on the job. We need to look at the total assignment we have given our employees and see what there is about it that will meet those needs. There are several steps we can go through to analyze the job: let's look at them one at a time.

First, are jobs clearly defined? Do the employees know exactly what is expected of them? Have we taken the time to go over each detail with each individual to be sure that he or she understands what is or isn't their responsibility? What about the interfaces between employees and departments? Does each employee know where his or her job stops and someone else's starts? Are their gaps or overlaps in the assignments?

We're talking about more than just a brief job description; we're talking about a comprehensive look at the job duties of each individual. Some jobs will be very

Chapter 8

clear and don't require much effort to analyze. Others have some complexities about them that require a careful look to determine exactly where the boundaries are between responsibilities.

Next, we should see if there are any parts of the job that could be done at a lower level because they require less skill than the others do. Are we asking a sales rep to fill out a mountain of reports that an admin assistant could easily handle allowing the sales rep to spend more time in front of their clients? Sometimes these things are best done by people with higher capabilities, but they rarely motivate those people or give them much of a feeling of accomplishment.

The way to measure these kinds of things is to ask ourselves, "Does it really take that person's talent to do that part of the job" Naturally there are some things in every job that are below the skill level of the employee doing it, but the important thing is to see just how much of the *total* time is being spent on these things versus how much on those things requiring more skill, judgment, experience, etc.

If the lesser jobs are using up too much time, then they should be removed or a different individual should be placed on the job is possible.

The next step is to look at where an employee's work comes from and where it goes when he or she is through with it. Too often employees find themselves taking work from some other person or department, doing some operation then passing it on to someone else.

Chapter 8

The Manager's Responsibility

We need to look at our own actions, too, in trying to enrich the job. Are we still doing part of the job that should be done by those under us? There is a good chance that if we came to our job from the one below us, we're still doing more of our old job than we should. Just because we're good at it doesn't justify not training someone else to do it.

The real test of our managerial skill is to see if we can quickly separate ourselves from doing those things that others are paid to do and tackle those things that *we* are paid to do.

It doesn't come easy. We all look for satisfaction from our jobs. Since managing is a hard job and the responsibilities sometimes aren't very clear, we tend to get frustrated early in our managerial career.

Trying to overcome this frustration often leads us to find satisfaction in working with *things* instead of *people*. This means we may start working on the equipment once in awhile, anything to get a little satisfaction of accomplishment. But we should remember; every time we do these things, we're admitting a little bit of failure. We're trying to enrich our jobs at the expense of those under us who should be doing these things.

Managers have to look for things that will enrich the jobs under them, even if it means reorganizing the work or shifting responsibilities. They have to recognize that not every job can be enriched, nor can every employee accept

Chapter 8

an equal amount of responsibility. Each employee has to *earn* the right to whatever responsibility is added to his or her job. Too often, we get the process backwards; we give the responsibility when the employees haven't shown a willingness to accept it. We hope that in doing this we will motivate them. But under these circumstances they may see our action as increasing their wok rather than responsibility. We will do better to reward the acceptance of responsibility. Note the difference between the following two approaches:

> "John, up until now I've been handling this. From now on I'm making this your responsibility."

> "John, since you've been making the decisions on this already and I've just been signing it, from now on would you like to send it out directly without my looking at it?"

In the first case it sounds like more work, even a little bit of a threat. The second case comes out as a reward for achievement and recognition of acceptable performance, but with an opportunity for John to decline if he doesn't want to do it.

Avoid 'More Work'

One of the reasons for rewarding acceptable performance is that when we begin to reorganize the work we are likely to do it along the lines of each individual's capabilities. The problem comes when we look at a job and say, "I need to give this person more responsibility," then assign more of the *same kind of work* he or she is already doing.

Chapter 8

What we have done is enlarged or expanded the job, not enriched it.

Project Motivation

Strangely enough, if we try to motivate our people by giving them more responsibility, we may find that we have left ourselves wide open to criticism. Suppose, for example, that our admin assistant Terri does a great job of responding to certain types of inquiries. Her knowledge of the subject is excellent as is her judgment.

We realize that she is only checking with us as a matter of routine. She makes the right decision, clears it with us, then handles the matter to completion. But there are times when we are out of the office or in a meeting and the action stops until we are able to give our approval. Here is an excellent chance to enrich her job. We see that she has earned the right to make her own decisions and to handle the matter without our even being involved. So we offer her the recognition of doing the entire thing without our approval. If she agrees, all evidence point to her doing an even better job, because it really is *her* job now.

But now a problem arises. Unless those above us are in agreement with what we are doing, we may get into hot water. Everything is fine as long as she makes the *right* decision, but what happens when something goes out that is wrong or is contrary to policy? When we are called in by those above us to explain the action and reason for the error, we have a choice of blaming Terri or accepting the blame ourselves. It may not be enough to say, "I was trying to motivate her," because the obvious questions

Chapter 8

then is, "Why does she need motivating? I thought she was a good employee."

It's just as bad to say, "I've been letting her make those decisions because when I am out of the office, there's no one to give approval." The response could be, "Maybe you're not doing *your* job by being away too much." The whole point of this is that there are some risks involved in giving recognition to those who have demonstrated their ability to achieve. It really cannot succeed unless those above us are aware of the principles involved and agree to go along with our efforts. The worst thing that could come out of this is for our boss to say, "This nearly got us into trouble, so from now on I want you to check everything that goes out." By the same reasoning, our boss could justify checking everything we do and having his or her boss check everything he or he does and continue up the line. Once such requests are put into place, they are difficult to remove.

Things that Motivate

We've talked about level of needs and the importance of letting the motivation come from the job itself. Perhaps it would be good to take a look at several things that are frequently used to motivate people and see just how each of them fits with the other in regards to satisfying and dissatisfying people. Let's compare the more commonly used actions and areas.

Achievement. This is simply the knowledge that we've done a good job and can step back and take a look at the finished product and know it's ours. Achievement is one

Chapter 8

of the highest satisfiers we have available to us, but there is a problem. It doesn't last very long. As soon as the employees start a new project, the achievement value of the last one is gone. Employees aren't very dissatisfied when they don't achieve and won't complain about not finishing something worthwhile, but they will be happy to see and hear that they have done something through to a satisfactory end.

Recognition / Status. As we've seen, status or recognition for having something others don't have – something perceived as valuable – is a strong need in everyone. When we recognize somebody for doing a better job than the others, we give them a good motivation boost. On the other hand, the absence of recognition makes people unhappy. People frequently complain that, "Nobody knows I exist around here." They'll also say something like, "I'm just part of the crowd – what I do isn't really that important." But if we tell them they've done a good job, let them know they're important or send them an email about a job well done, they will have a complete attitude turnaround.

Responsibility. Being responsible for something is important to most people and strangely enough, it is mostly a *matter of perception*. We don't even have to change the job to make people feel they have responsibility. When someone comes in the office to ask for information, all we have to so say is, "Ask Mark; he's responsible for that." When Mark hears that we think he's responsible for the activity, he'll be much more motivated than if we answered the question ourselves. As a motivator, responsibility lasts longer than most other things.

Chapter 8

The Job Itself. We've already talked about the importance of the nature of the work as far as motivation is concerned, but let's get it into perspective. More than anything else, the nature of the work and the responsibility we have for that work motivates us to continue to work well. If the work is satisfying, meaningful and something over which the employees have some control, they will continue to be motivated over a long period of time. However, the absence of meaningful work and responsibility aren't necessarily things that make them unhappy. We won't hear employees demanding more responsibilities or more demanding work, but in the absence of these things they are much more likely to complain about working conditions, wages or their boss.

Advancement / Promotion. Moving up to another job or acquiring more duties in the present job is a form of recognition and a very good motivator. The promotion is not something that motivates employees, everyday, but that's okay as we are not in the position to give out promotions to everyone every day. We can give some other forms of recognition and praise more frequently, so we depend on those forms more than we do on advancements. However, we shouldn't rule out promotions as motivation opportunities. The prospect of getting a higher rated job or promotion is real and it serves to get more work from people as they see the reality of the prospect getting closer to them.

Money / Security. These, too, are tricky things. Since it is obvious that most people are working for money and some security, it is reasonable to assume that these are

Chapter 8

important motivators. However, since we are never able to pay them as much as they would like to have, they will always want more, spend more and feel they deserve more. The most important thing about this is for us to know that when the other important motivators like responsibility, recognition, achievement and the opportunity to do meaningful work are absent, no amount of money will continue to motivate people indefinitely.

Perhaps we can best understand the part these things play by dividing them into two kinds: *the money and security we don't have* and *the money and security we have just gotten*. In the first part, even though we don't have them, the anticipation of getting them will serve to motivate us. If we don't have them, don't get them or if other people have them, we're going to be unhappy. When we get it, we're happy for the moment. We're even happier if we get more than we expected or more than others got. In either case, whether we do or do not have money and security, we think about it every time we get a paycheck. If the amount is to our liking, we're motivated. If not, we're unhappy.

Working Conditions. We hear a lot of complaints about poor working conditions. How good a motivator are good working conditions? Over the years we've found out that most often when employees are complaining about working conditions, something is missing. Usually we find that if they aren't getting much satisfaction from their jobs, they will notice the long hours or temperature levels. When we have employees doing a job they like and have a commitment to, they rarely complain about the working conditions, unless there's something about the

Chapter 8

conditions that prevents them from getting their job done.

What does all of this tell us? Mostly it says that people don't always know what makes them happy and unhappy. It tells us that there are things we can do to motivate people. We can give responsibility, since it is often only a matter of the employee's perception of the job. We can give recognition to let the employee know that achievement has been reached. We can make the job meaningful by letting the employee know why it's important and by letting them know they have responsibility for the end results. Interestingly enough, none of these things cost money. The other things, which actually motivate less, cost money; so we have within our power the chance to motivate employees without going for more money, higher salaries and without spending a lot of money and time on improving working conditions.

Production – Minded Management

It really wouldn't be right to leave a chapter on motivation – where we've spent so much time talking about how we can enrich the job, how we can do things for the employees to motivate them and how much responsibility we have as managers to enrich their jobs – without addressing *production*. When it comes right down to it, getting out the work or the service is what it's all about. It's why there are employees and why there are managers. Hospitals and service organizations have to give good service. They have to think about saving money. Any non-profit organization can exist only when

Chapter 8

their directors feel that the service being given is up to the standard of expectations for the amount of budget it takes to offer that service. Profit-centered organizations understand this at management levels. It may not be understood at lower levels. Even front line managers may be so closely tied to the working units that they miss the point that production is the reason there is any profit at all.

We have to understand that 'saving money' and making a profit *aren't bad words*. And they *aren't bad reasons* for working effectively.

Whatever style the manager finally develops, it must take in account that if the employees don't produce, something will have to be done. This doesn't suggest that we aren't interested in the employee and that we don't try hard to provide means of motivation. In fact, it means just the opposite.

We do all of these things because we've seen that they produce motivated workers and motivated workers produce more. The manager must keep in mind that just keeping the employee happy on the job or making the organization a good place to work isn't the end of the matter. The end of it all is to get the most production from the fewest people with the best product or service that we can offer. In a profit-making organization, it also means making it better and / or cheaper than the competition.

What do we do as a result of this knowledge of the need for production? We watch the results in terms of production, *not employee satisfaction alone.* If we

Chapter 8

believe the idea that people are likely to respond with more production when they believe in the job, then we do whatever we can to enrich their jobs and make them meaningful and show how the jobs contribute to the overall picture. We'll also watch production figures and job standards and see if we're on target. We'll see how many calls the sales force is making; we'll see how many cases are handled; we'll see how many customers are being waited on. We'll pass this information on to the employees as *their reason for being there*. We'll also show our dissatisfaction when we continually fall short of the goals that we have set.

Finally, we have to understand that the front line manager is closer than anyone else in the organization to the major causes and the means of prevention of cost inflation. To see this, we have to recognize the typical inflationary pattern:

> Wages increase
> Cost of material increases
> Time to produce a product or service remains the same or increases
> Production of product or service increases slightly or not at all

When these four elements exist – and it doesn't take all four of them – we have inflation. That means we have to pay more for the same thing. And that means we go back to our employer and ask for a 'cost of living' increase. And *that* means it's going to cost our employer *more* to provide the *same* service or product. So, prices will have to be raised and the spiral will continue.

Chapter 8

It will always continue under these circumstances until one thing happens: *Production goes up* – and far enough to offset the increased costs. If we get more production for the same amount, we can even *lower* the price and the users of the service or product can get *more* for their money instead of less. This is the way to stop inflation. The front line manager has to constantly think of ways to get more production from the same people, or get the same production at a lower cost – or both. An alternative would be to improve the product or service, so that when the customer pays more, they get more for their money. However, the best option may be to hold down the cost of the product or service that has already proven satisfactory.

Employee Involvement

We are all more likely to be committed to things we're involved in and we're more likely to believe in and support things into which we've had some input. That's what we've been saying about motivating people by enriching the job to the extent it is meaningful to the employee. What can the manager do to get their group involved?

He or she can get their employees together, individually or collectively and ask them honestly what can be done to improve whatever it is that needs improving. Let the employees have some time to work on it, then try to use their findings and give them credit for it. It takes very little effort on our part to ask an employee what he or she thinks is the problem in a particular situation; we can even make it an interesting assignment to find out.

Chapter 8

For example, "Sue, we're really having a problem getting these reports out on time, aren't we. Why don't you think about it for a couple of days, and then let's get back together and see what you think we can do. I'm sure you're closer to the problem than I am, so you will probably have a better idea of how to solve it than I will. By the way, if you need any information other help, feel free to ask around." In about 30 seconds of conversation, we've set the stage for some *work improvement.*

We can repeat this with any of our employees, for any problem we may have. Just think how nice it would be if all our employees were working to make their jobs better and all we had to do is sit back and wait for them to show up with their suggestions. Of course, it's not quite that simple, but the principle is. The worst thing that can happen is that they don't think of any suggestions and that is no different from where we were when we asked. At least they had a *chance* to contribute and that should serve as some motivation in itself. The worst thing we can do is assume that our employees really aren't interested. If we decide for them that they don't know anything about improving, we will never tap into this very valuable resource.

Team Building

One of the benefits that come from having the employees work on trying to improve things in the workplace is that they often become an efficient and cohesive team. They work together, solve problems together, engage in some give and take activity and gradually find themselves liking to work together. There are other things that help produce this result, most of which can be initiated by the

Chapter 8

manager, since they basically revolve around the *environment* when the work is taking place. Perhaps it would be better to describe it as the 'workplace atmosphere'. For example, is it pleasant to work here or is there a lot of bickering and bitterness? Is it a good idea to forget any suggestions or is management receptive to new ideas? Is knowledge a source of power or do people share their information freely – do managers give information to their subordinates? Do people distrust each other, do the workers distrust the managers, do the managers distrust the workers or is there a real trust among all the people?

The answers to these and many more questions are good indicators of just how much team building has been done in the organization. The 'work atmosphere' is not good just because we have nice people around. It happens because we carefully and openly work at creating an atmosphere or environment where these positive things can develop to some degree. Some have suggested that looking at both the good and bad signs like those we've just mentioned is a good way to measure the health of an organization.

Review

As we suggested in the last chapter, when we were talking about directing people, leadership in the world of management is different from the rest of the world's idea of leadership. So is motivation. Many think that to motivate people is to stir them up to the point where they go charging out and work themselves into exhaustion just because their leader has inspired them so much. In management, the idea is to get the employees involved in

Chapter 9

fulfilling enough of their own needs through the things the job offers so that they get satisfaction from doing their job. When the job is challenging enough, meaningful enough and gives them enough recognition, managers don't have to offer any motivation. The managers' job is to make sure the job offers all of those things.

There's not much that will motivate a person more than having responsibility for some specific tasks that are well defined and well recognized. But not everyone deserves or can take responsibility. It should be given as a reward – and only when those it's offered to, agree to take the consequences of failure as well as the rewards of success.

This means the employees must have the *right to make mistakes*, to be wrong as well as the *right to be right*. It means that when we give responsibility as a way of creating motivation, we can't check everything that goes out and correct the errors. If we check everything, we've only left the employee the right to be right. If errors are stopped by us, the employee will never have to live with the mistakes – and the consequences of those mistakes.

If the employee knows he or she will have to live with consequences, the end result is an employee who works much harder *at being right* and who is very motivated.

Chapter 9

Interviewing Skills

When we talk with employees about specific things, such as telling them how they are doing, correcting some fault in their work performance or trying to assist them in solving some problem, we call this interviewing. This is one more technique the new manager needs to learn and the more we do it, the better we get at it. The problem is we don't really do much interviewing every day, so even the most experienced managers can get rusty. The best thing we can do is to look at the techniques required, practice them whenever we can, think about each interview we conduct and practice the techniques each time we have an interview.

In this chapter, we will talk about the general principles of conducting any type of interview, then look as some specific kinds, namely Employment, Counseling,

Chapter 9

Disciplinary, Appraisal and Exit. As we have said, interviewing is not an everyday occurrence for the manager, so we can't really expect to be experts, but since there are some basic points we can remember, it's good to review them every once in a while. We name them so we can talk about them separately, but actually we find ourselves combining them at times, as we will see further on.

General Principles

Basically there are three general purposes of an interview – to *predict behavior*, as in the case of an employment interview, where we want to know how well we think the potential employee will do on the job; to *change behavior* where it isn't meeting a standard, such as the disciplinary interview when the employee is constantly late or below production standard or has an attitude that is affecting the behavior of others; or to *establish exactly what the behavior is*, as in the appraisal interview.

When we are preparing for an interview, we need to decide which of the purposes we have in mind for it. Why are we having it, why are we having it now and why are we having it with this particular person? But we need to establish not only why we are having it, but also what we hope to *accomplish* in the interview. If the purpose is to change behavior, do we know what specific behavior we want? Once we have decided what we want or don't want, we need to know how we are going to get the person to change. And we should know whether we expect the total change to be made as a result of this interview, or whether there will be more later.

Chapter 9

The best thing to do before an interview is to write ourselves a note stating the purpose of the interview, where we're going, why we're going these and we expect to get there. This has the advantage of making us organize our thoughts and may even convince us that this is not the time to have the interview, or that we need to talk to all of our people, or that we need more information. At least it will give us an opportunity to spend a few moments analyzing the situation before we get into it.

Establishing the Proper Climate

Interviewing is talking *with* people – not talking *to* people or talking *at* people. Talking with people means that *we listen twice as much as we talk*. It means that the other person has something to say and a right to say it. When the interview is over, we can be sure it was a bad one if our reflections show us that we did most of the talking. This tells us that we did the talking and he or she did the listening. On the other hand, we can probably say that is was a good interview if we got a lot of information and the interviewee did a lot of talking. So listening is one of the things we must determine to do.

We must determine to be fair. Part of deciding to be fair in our interviews is to admit that there is always the chance that the interviewees might be right. At least there is the possibility that they could be more right than we are. This doesn't mean that we are going against the established facts. It means that we are willing to admit that our employees have some right on their side and we are willing to hear them out. One good way to approach the interview is to try to put ourselves in the interviewees'

Chapter 9

position and view the situation from their standpoint, even if we think the situation is an extreme one. Another part of determining to be fair is deciding how we will let interviewees know we want to be that way. The best way to convince them is to *show* them, not tell them. When they say something we listen and accept what they say. We refer to it later to let them know that we listened. We give a chance to defend themselves or to state more facts or disagree with us all in a threat-free situation.

We start our interviews by letting the interviewees know that we want to talk to them under the best conditions. When they come in we greet them in such a manner as to let them know we were expecting them and are planning to talk and listen.

We don't say, "Wait a few minutes until I finish these important things and then we'll talk." While we probably wouldn't say it this way, we can easily leave that impression by continuing to work while the interviewee stands and watches. We greet them and show that they come first by making sure our email and phones are turned off so that no one will interrupt us. We seat the interviewees comfortably, not in awkward position where they have to turn to see us or with direct sunlight shining in their eyes. It's often a good idea to come out from behind our desk and sit beside them or at the corner of your desk, to avoid having the desk act as a barrier between you.

Any time we are talking with people it makes good sense to open the conversation on a light topic instead of jumping right to the point. Our opening remarks should show an interest in our interviewee, their families or their

Chapter 9

hobbies. This shouldn't be forced, it should be with genuine interest, but most importantly, it shouldn't be too long. Interviewees know we want to talk to them so the sooner we get to the subject, the sooner they will begin to relax. We are the manager, in our office, so we should take the lead as soon as appropriate and start talking about the subject of the interview. "David, I called you in so we could go over your question about..." This gets us started and no one is surprised. This way David knows quickly what the subject is about and can get his thoughts in order. He knows why he's there, what we expect him to discuss and can give us information without guessing. After all, we want him to be free to speak and to give us as much good, usable information as possible. This can only happen if he knows what we're talking about.

As we have said, the interview is as much a listening routine as a talking one for us. We give full attention to the answers to our questions. We listen when interviewees talk. We consider their remarks, answer their questions the best we can, but keep the interview focused on the topic at hand.

One of the errors most often committed is to let those being interviewed get us off the subject and cause us to discuss things that we really hadn't prepared to talk about. When our time is up, we discover that we haven't covered the material we wanted to talk about and either, have to schedule another interview or make this one go longer than we intended. But if we have directed the interview properly, we should close without letting it drag on. Once we've gotten the information we wanted, answered the interviewees' questions or settled the

Chapter 9

problem, the wisest thing to do is to end the session as quickly and politely as possible. One good way for us to close and also to get a little feedback from them is to ask them to sum up the findings as they see them. This way we can see if they have any misunderstandings about the things that have been discussed and also to let them know that the interview is over. If there is any action to be taken, state that clearly, as well as who will do the action:

> "I'll call you Thursday to review"

> "We'll try it for a month then talk again"

> "You call me when you've decided what you want to do about the job."

We should remember to let the interviewee leave on the same friendly note they came in on, regardless of the outcome of the interview. Even if there is a disagreement, there is no need to be disagreeable.

The Employment Interview

Often the job of interviewing new or prospective employees is not the job of the new manager, but its well to know some of the techniques just the same. Even if the HR department or someone higher than us makes the final decision on who we hire, we still may have to interview the individual to decide exact job placement or to give our final approval. If there is a possibility that the individual will end up working for us, we should *want* to interview the person, not try to avoid it. Let's examine why this interview is so important to us, the individual and the organization.

Chapter 9

Any time we add someone to our organization, we are in the process of trying to match a person and a job. There is a good chance that we are starting someone on a career. We are saying that this person has the unique qualifications to fit the particular job, or at least the potential to grow into it. In a way, the individual is relying on us to decide whether or not he or she is suited for the job. When we ask the typical questions like: "Well, do you think you will fit into this job"? or "How do you think you will like this work?" we are asking unfair questions. If we've done our interview correctly, we are in a better position to know the answers than the applicant has. We know the job and we should know him or her pretty well by now. All of these are reasons why the interview is important from the applicant's standpoint. From the organization's standpoint it's equally important. It's much easier to get an employee on the payroll than off of it. We should do the hiring very carefully. Sometimes the organization may pass employees around from one job to another trying to find something they can do, all because they shouldn't have been hired in the first place. Whoever made the mistake in hiring them has cost the organization considerable money and wasted time. We need to be sure we do our job of interviewing carefully so this can't be said about us a few years from now.

When we conduct employment interviews we should be certain of their purpose. Primarily, there are two basic things we want to accomplish: *give information* and *get information*. Perhaps the *getting* of information is the most important. What kind of information do we want to get? We want to get whatever past employment history

Chapter 9

we can. We need to find out what skills our prospective employees have used, not just which ones they have. How much growth have they shown? What kind of promotions or advancements did they have on their last job? How stable are they as employees? Does this one have a history of moving from one job to another or has he or she had one or two jobs over several years? Such questions as "What did you do to develop in your last assignment?" will tell us a lot if we listen carefully enough.

Asking questions is a good way to find out about the interviewees' attitude toward management too. Is this one aggressive, not wanting to be managed? Is that one easily disgruntled? Adaptable? "What kind of bosses do you like best?" "Tell me about some of your good managers." "What bothers you the most about bosses?"

These aren't trick questions; the answers should give us useful information. We aren't playing games and we should let employees know that. If one says she likes bosses that leave her alone, let her make mistakes as well as get credit for a job well done, then she may have the makings of an excellent employee. If another says he likes bosses to give him clear directions and kept him posted along the way, we may find that he isn't aggressive as we would like, especially if the job is one that may require individual thinking. And if others give us a series of stories about managers who didn't understand them, or who picked on them all the time, we may find that it won't be long before we fall into that same category – hearing complaints about how we pick on them.

Chapter 9

It's always wise for us to inquire about the personal ambitions of our potential employees. Where do they expect to go in the organization? How high up do they feel their capacity for responsibility and authority might take them? We need to know whether they're going to be willing to learn the jobs one at a time, or expect to move up rapidly without really finding out what's going on. We should try to find out whether they will be content to work satisfactorily on one job without a promise of promotion. We can ask the interviewees how they see themselves preparing for a career. We can ask what part they think experience plays in their development. We aren't likely to get exact answers, but we will get some good indicators. Our ability to interpret the answers will grow as we get more experience, but it isn't as hard as it may sound. *The key is still our ability to listen.*

To the second major purpose of the employment interview is to *give* information. Prospective employees need to know something about the organization, *but not everything.* They need to know something about the policies, objectives, restrictions and benefits that will most affect them and that apply to them. Automatic pay increases, bonuses and paid vacations probably mean much more to a young single person than the health benefits and retirement plan.

Accomplishments of the organization, provisions for the family and promotion opportunities mean much more to the mature person looking for a career. But this isn't the time to oversell the organization. While we don't have to accentuate the weaknesses, we don't have to pretend the place is perfect either. Above all, be honest, especially if interviewees ask specific questions. It's better for them to

Chapter 9

know about any restrictive policies now than to find them out later on by surprise.

Part of the reason for giving out information is to let interviewees know about the job they will be doing. Again, honesty is the rule. If there is likely to be much overtime, say so. If the job is routine at times don't be afraid to mention it; at the same time, point out the more exciting features as well. If interviewees aren't likely to understand the terminology, don't spend a lot of time going into great details about the job. Let them ask questions after you have given them enough information to make their questions meaningful. It's even a good idea to 'help' them ask questions. "Do you have any questions about the operation?" Is there something that I can give you more information about?" Let them know about what their salary and vacation schedule would be and make it clear in exact terms. It is often a good idea to advise of all payroll deductions so that they aren't surprised when they get their first paycheck. If they are entitled to a full vacation with pay in their first year, be sure they know it. Don't leave it up to them to ask such important questions.

If interviewees ask about the future, we answer them to the best of our ability, but obviously we shouldn't promise them anything that we aren't sure we can deliver. Perhaps the best thing to do is let them see what others have done with backgrounds and experience similar to theirs. But since it's an interview, it's a good idea to get their views, their ideas and their questions about the future. Find out where they see themselves going and how fast they want to get there. "Where do you think your skills and talents will best direct you in our business?"

Chapter 9

This kind of question will always give us some insight into interviewees' hopes and aspirations. They must realize that the future depends as much on them as on the organization, so questions that will let us know how they are likely to relate to the organization and the people around them will give us more information. The questions should be worded correctly, though, or the answers won't give very meaningful information. Asking, "Do you get along with people?" is a question we won't get properly answered as it is too direct. If we try asking it this way, "Tell me about some of the people you didn't get along with very well in your last job." This is a leading question, but we haven't supplied the interviewee with any clues as to the *right* answer, so they must answer from their own ideas and feelings.

The Counseling Interview

Sometimes employees have problems and the result is that we find ourselves involved in counseling interviews. Since the problems may be of the emotional type, these interviews will differ from the others we will have. The approach will be different, too. Most often, counseling interviews have come about as a result of employees coming to us, rather than our going to them. Because of this we are seen in a different light. We don't have the same kind of controls on the time or duration or topics to be discussed, etc. as we do in the other type of interviews.

As managers, we are concerned about the employees' well being, of course, but we are also concerned with their performance. If their problems affect their performance on the job, we have to help them or resolve those

Chapter 9

problems in some way to protect the organization as well as the individual. Most personal problems are not job related, but if they have a bad effect on job performance, most employees will realize it. They'll know that they aren't doing as well as they are capable of doing and this just compounds their worries, making the original problem worse. For this reason, if it is at all possible, we should help our employees solve whatever personal problems they bring us without any reference to job performance. This in itself may make them feel a little better and more capable of dealing with other things.

Employees may not even know the cause of their problems. They may have some family problems that cause them to come to work in a bad frame of mind, or may cause them to interpret things in the wrong light, or may even cause them to say and do things that create problems for other around them. They may have financial problems that cause them to worry and fail to concentrate on their job. Their lack of concentration may create safety problems or cut into production schedules. It may cause errors that show up much later in our operation. One of the serious consequences of employees' worrying about financial problems may be that they will get all kinds of delusions about what their salary should be, how much overtime they should get and what kind of intervals they should have between raises.

Help Them Out

When employees come to us with problems, there are two approaches we can take, each quite different from each other. We can assume responsibility for the problems. We can take the whole load on our shoulders, look for

Chapter 9

solutions, get information for the employees and offer to go as far as we can to do whatever is necessary to solve the problems for them. As undesirable as this sounds, there are times when we would go this far. When an employee comes to us apparently unwilling or unable to face the problem squarely, we need to step in and give support. Obviously we don't take over permanently, but in time of stress the employee needs to know that somebody who cares is able to help them. We also shouldn't step in and take over the problem just because it's been brought to us. Part of the problem may be that the employee is unwilling to recognize the problem as his or her fault and may be trying to place the responsibility on someone else. For us to step in and take over would be the worst thing to do.

The other extreme from our taking over is to let the employee take the responsibility entirely upon him or herself. We just listen. We may make a statement like, "That's interesting" but do nothing. As unlikely as it seems there are times when this is exactly the right approach.

When the employee shows he or she has the strength to face the problem but wants a sympathetic ear we would do a lot of harm if we took over. All of us like to have someone to talk to now and then. We aren't necessarily looking for advice. We aren't even expecting the person we're talking with to agree or disagree with us. We just find that we understand our problem better at the end of the conversation. So it is when an employee comes to us with a problem and appears to just want to talk, our best response is to let him or her do just that.

Chapter 9

Ideally, of the two options, the one that allows the employees to take responsibility for their problems is the best. Even if we start off by taking over, we should also immediately begin to look for ways to return the responsibility to them. Gradually we shift it back by asking questions and letting the employees supply the answers instead of the other way around. As they begin to take the responsibility again. We keep them on the right track by asking the right questions – questions that simply make them face another truth or help them avoid the wrong conclusion – and step in only when they appear to be in trouble. The important thing is to get the problem solved and not get the credit for solving it. The thing that may make the solution most effective is our ability to convince the employee that it was his or her solution.

Finally, keep employees' problems confidential, if possible. Avoid putting those problems into their personnel records, especially when they have come to you expecting to get private help. If there was a discussion about performance, or the meeting resulted from a performance problem, then it may be necessary to put this in the files.

If appraisal records are open to other managers, we should be careful about putting anything about this meeting in those records unless employees are agreeable to it. Another caution is to avoid casually mentioning the problem to other managers. If we give up the confidence that has been given to us, we will not only aggravate the problem, but we can be sure we've had our last counseling interview.

Chapter 9

The Disciplinary Interview

Counseling interviews are difficult because they are different from other types of interviews. Disciplinary interviews are difficult because they have the potential of being very unpleasant. They are one of those necessary evils that managers have as part of their job. The disciplinary interview is a basic requirement of our job and rarely ever is as bad as we expect it to be. The reason we have these interviews is that employees break rules.

We have to have rules and regulations – standards of the job – but rules get broken. Not everyone meets every standard all the time. When employees fail too often or by too great a margin to meet the standard, we have to discipline them – or *change the standard*. We simply can't run an organization in which people continually fail to meet the standards set by those in the highest positions. Nothing lowers morale more quickly or destroys our effectiveness as a manager more completely than allowing someone to constantly break the organization's rules.

If we set a precedent by letting one person get away with something, we have little chance of stopping others who decide to try the same thing. It's equally hard on the person who wants to abide by the rules when everyone else is allowed to do otherwise. Even when it's only one person who habitually comes in late, if the office hours are established and accepted, then everyone should abide by them – no exceptions.

When considering the disciplinary interview, the simplest way is to take a *positive* attitude toward it. For the good

Chapter 9

of all concerned, something needs to be done. If the problem is allowed to continue, nothing but trouble can result. The organization is suffering because of the situation and to let something get worse because we don't want to do something unpleasant doesn't make good sense.

Not only is the organization not functioning at its best, but our job is harder because of the problem and we, too, are failing to operate as well as we can. We are having to cover up or make excuses or explain to others because of the situation that one employee has gotten us into, so we have every right to attack the problem head-on. We have already seen that the others in the group are going to become involved, especially if the situation is allowed to continue without corrective action, so for the good of the others in the work group we need to do something quickly.

Even the employees who cause the problems suffer from them. Their careers are in jeopardy, because the longer this goes on, the worse we may think of them – perhaps even wore than they deserve. So, regardless of how unpleasant the interview may appear, the reasons for doing it are real. If we do a good job of it and get the problem solved, we will be the stronger for it and all concerned will be happier and better workers as a result.

But two things are worthy of a special note here: No matter how much we want to avoid the confrontation, it won't get any easier if we put it off. Second, this kind of interview is rarely as bad as we expect it to be.

Chapter 9

The Process

Disciplinary interviews begin just like the others we have talked about. Our first action is to put our interviewees at ease, going through the steps we have discussed. The worst thing we can do is jump all over them the minute they walk into the office. If we feel that our temper is going to explode, then we had better call off the interview until we calm down. We must continually remind ourselves that all employees are valuable and we shouldn't do anything that will cause them to become less valuable.

We aren't trying to win a battle – we're trying to get the organization back to running the way it should. We aren't trying to prove any points or who is wrong and who is right. We are simply trying to correct a situation that cannot be allowed to continue. Our employees must know that we are trying to be fair. From the moment we begin talking to them, they must recognize this. Being fair means that we want to hear their side of the matter and want to know any facts they might have to add to the total knowledge we have.

We must have as much information as possible before we start the interview.

This brings up an important point: We must have as much information as possible before we start the interview. Perhaps more than any other kind of interview, the disciplinary interview requires that we be fully informed. This is no time to discover that we have our

Chapter 9

facts wrong or that we don't have the whole story. And it's just as important to remember to have the facts verified. When we say, "You've been late nearly every day this month," we aren't really making a hard, factual statement. We would do much better to have the exact information and say, "You've been late 14 days this month." The difference between the two statements is the difference between confidence and shaky ground.

We must also be sure that the interviewees know they're being disciplined. Sometimes we catch ourselves trying to sneak the disciplinary comments in between praising comments and the interviewees lose the message. If we wait until they're about to leave and then say, "By the way..." and go into the reasons for calling the meeting, we've done both them and ourselves an injustice. They should know from the start that this is the purpose of the interview.

They should know that their behavior has been unacceptable. We should tell them what the standard is and where they have failed to meet it. Just as clearly, we should let them know what corrections are expected and when they should take place. Of course, this isn't a "tell, tell, tell" interview. Once we have stated the reason for the interview – we need to "listen, listen, listen." We want to be sure the interviewees have a chance to state their side of the story.

There is always the possibility that they may have some things in their favor that we haven't considered. If someone says, "My last boss told me that it was alright," or "The other departments started doing this, two months

Chapter 9

ago," we had better be prepared to study the matter further. At least we should know if these things are true.

Finally, we should deal with employees' specific problems, not their total performance – unless their total performance is in question. There's little to be gained by making interviewees look worse that they really are just to prove a point. We need to be ready to admit their strengths and be willing to praise them as the occasion arises.

But we can't let the good points overshadow the bad, nor can we hide the fact that they are being called in to answer for their conduct. Like most interviews, the disciplinary one needs to terminate with the same preciseness with which it began.

The longer we drag it out the more danger there is that we will begin to cloud the issue. We need to deal with the problem, state the standard, state the acceptable behavior we expect from the employee, listen to all the facts, answer questions, be sure that he or she understands what happens now – then end the interview. If possible, we end on a positive note of our expectations for better performance; we end on a pleasant note to show we expect things to work out; and most importantly – we end it.

The Appraisal Interview

When we appraise our people, we generally end up with an interview to discuss the matter with them. This is called an appraisal interview. It should be done periodically for the benefit of the employee and ourselves.

Chapter 9

They need to know their strengths and weaknesses and we need to know how they see themselves and the job. But if the organization has a regularly scheduled time for making appraisals then we must observe this. However, we shouldn't wait until that one time a year to let our people know how they are doing. If we expect smooth development of the people who work for us, we must let them know as often as possible where they need to grow.

Once a year isn't often enough. The appraisal interview isn't something that's done once a year to satisfy some organizational policy; it's something that we do with our employees as often as we need to discuss their growth and development.

The primary purpose of the appraisal interview is to get a comprehensive look at employees as they fit into the organization and how they fit into it in the future. It should be the most enjoyable of all sessions we have with the employees, because it's a time to help employees grow. This isn't the time to point out faults and we don't bring out any disciplinary items we may have. The purpose of the interview should be clear in our minds and clear to the employees.

Employee Participation

Employees should be given the chance to be a part of every interview, but especially this one. They should know in advance that the interview is planned. They should know that we want them to participate and that we will be talking about the *future* as well as the past. Of course, each interview starts with putting the employee at ease, but this one shouldn't take as long as the others.

Chapter 9

Most employees want to know how well we think they are doing and are anxious to get to the subject, especially if they know in advance that we want to talk about their progress. As soon as we get into the subject, we should let the employees tell us how they see themselves and how they see their jobs.

By doing a brief task analysis they let us know what they think their job is, which may explain why they have certain shortcomings – there may be things that they just don't know they're supposed to do. As we begin to compare our views with those of the interviewees, we need to be careful that they don't lose sight of the fact that we want them to be part of the discussion. If we become too dominate, they'll begin to think that we already have our minds made up and anything they say won't make a difference.

So we try to keep them in the conversation throughout the entire interview. We give them the honest impression that this is their session, their opportunity to get the facts on how they're doing and where they're going. When they see something differently from the way we see it, their opinion should be as good as ours. If they have the supporting data, then we should accept what they say.

In the appraisal interview we should concentrate on the future as much as possible. Even when we're talking about past performance, we want it to relate to the employees' future performance. How can they change to do things better? What are they doing now that is great and likely to enhance their chances for a promotion in the future? As much as possible, we should let them set their own goals and decide what action plans will produce the

Chapter 9

best results for them and the organization. They should be allowed to participate in setting objectives for themselves and selecting any corrective action that is decided on. As we look at the interviewees' future, we help them set both long and short range goals for themselves.

The long range goals will deal with their ambitions and their direction in the organization. The short range goals will have to do only with the job at hand. We will want to help them see that there is a certain danger in looking too far ahead, especially if they begin to forget about the obligations of their present job. Too many people have failed in the future because they didn't give enough attention to the present.

Part of our obligation as a manager is to let the employees know how they are doing on their present assignment so they have an opportunity to make the most of the future. The appraisal interview allows us an excellent opportunity to do this, especially if we let the employees be a part of setting the short and long range objectives for themselves.

As in any interview, we should be sure the employees know exactly what we are saying. We should state how we see their job and their future. As their interview gets close to the end, we should begin to summarize and clear up any misunderstandings that have arisen. If we have decided on some specific training or other course of action, we should state that clearly. If there is some follow up required, then the time and place should be confirmed.

Chapter 9

Even if another meeting isn't scheduled, we should establish that we don't want to wait until next year to talk about the interviewee's progress and future. Employees should always feel free to talk with us and equally free to initiate such a meeting.

Finally, we should note that some employees may take our appraisal efforts as just another chance to criticize them. They may not accept the things that we say. They may not agree with our evaluation of them. They may rationalize and blame the organization or other members of the group around them. If we do our best and the situation still turns out this way, then we may have actually found out more about these employees than we already knew.

We now know that they can't take criticism and they lack the ability to see themselves as others see them. If so, then so be it. We've done our part and we will continue to do our part. We'll continue to keep them involved in these interviews. We'll even look at our own information to see if it's faulty in some way.

But we must still be the manager and we must still do what's right. The worst thing we can do is to let the employee persuade us into changing our mind or actions. As we have said, employees want us to tell them how we see them, both now and in the future. If we have done a good job of preparing for the interview, we will be satisfied with the outcome and look forward to the next one.

Chapter 9

The Exit Interview

As a new manager, very few of us get the opportunity to conduct exit interviews, which are simply interviews with employees who have chosen to leave the organization. The purpose of these interviews isn't to try to persuade the employees to change their mind. Often managers do this and end up making things worse than when the employee decided to leave. So why have interviews with people who are leaving, especially if we aren't supposed to try to get them to stay with the organization?

The reasons are pretty obvious when we start to think about all the things we can learn from such interviews. As managers we need to check our perception. How well do we know the individuals that are leaving? Do we really know why they're leaving? Do we really know what their relationship is with the rest of the organization?

The answers to these questions should come out of the interviews – to check our perception. Another reason for exit interviews is to check our own abilities as managers. Have we got some weaknesses that could be corrected? Are we somehow at fault for the individual's leaving? Have we created a situation in the work group that may cause others to leave too? This, also, should come out of the interview.

Another reason for the interview is to check the organization's policies and working conditions. Are we matching the wrong people with our jobs? Are our hiring policies out of date or out of line with other organizations? Is there something wrong with our wage structure? The answers to these questions may not be

Chapter 9

found in one interview, but clues may be learned in the things that are found out. This is another reason for conducting exit interviews.

A final reason for these interviews is that they benefit the employees that are leaving. The may need to get some things off their chest. They may feel some remorse about leaving and the interview can help as they talk about the decision they have made. Most important, they may be heading into some future trouble which can be prevented by a calm and rational talk. All of these become real, logical and sound reasons for having the interview. But none of the results will be satisfactory if we a poor job of conducting the interviews.

How do we conduct exit interviews? In the beginning, this type looks similar to the others, but there are some important differences. As usual, we want to put the interviewees at ease and let them know that we appreciate their time in talking to us. We must immediately let them know that we feel that they can help us and would appreciate their help. And we want to assure them we are not going to try to change their minds. We want them to know that our intention is to *listen*. We are looking for insight into our own problems and ways that we can improve the organization. Above all, we should put the interviewees at ease by letting them know we aren't going to ask them to tell us any possible bad things about others in the group.

When an exit interview starts, *we start listening*. We ask open-ended questions designed to get the interviewees talking and *keep them talking*. We avoid interrupting them and we must not go on the defensive. We don't want

Chapter 9

it to become a 'policy defense' interview. We correct any statements about policy that are untrue, but we don't have to defend them. No matter how much we would like to launch into a statement about all the good things that these policies have accomplished, this isn't the time for us to be giving out information like that. We want to keep the disagreement to a minimum, so even when we correct a statement to supply the facts, we do it by saying, "Well, it may have appeared that way, but actually the policy reads..." And when we come to a situation where there is no way to avoid disagreement, we need to say, "It's interesting that you feel that way," not "You're crazy if that's the way you think it is."

Exit interviews have one hazard that we must be aware of and avoid. We must be sure not to let them degenerate into name calling sessions about the people in the group. Unless there is substantial amount of evidence, there is no need to get into a discussion about specific people. Even if evidence is presented, there is no reason to talk about people unless there is something useful to be gained by it. It makes more sense to talk only about those things that we can do something about. If the interviewees want to talk about something that bothered them while they were working, but it is something that shouldn't have affected them, then this too has no real place in the discussion.

Use the Information

In one respect, exit interviews are like all other interviews we have – we must learn to use the information we get. It's useless to take the time to gather information if we don't use it after we get it. Exit interviews may be the

Chapter 9

most important of all interviews. Using the information from them may be the means of preventing other exit interviews in the future. We should study the information and decide what we've really learned and how can we use it. If we have found a bad situation, we should correct it. If the information tells us that something we did caused a problem, we take the necessary steps to ensure it doesn't happen again. Finally, we should review our own actions during these interviews to see if we are satisfied with the way we conducted them. We ask ourselves:

"Did I plan it well?"

"Did I put the employee at ease?"

"Did it go as I had planned it?"

"Did I really accomplish anything?"

"How did the employee feel when it was over?"

"How did I feel when it was over?"

"If I had to do it over again, would I do it differently?"

If the answer to this last question is, "Yes", then we need to take whatever steps are necessary to ensure that we really do it differently the next time.

Review

Successful interviews don't just happen. They are carefully planned. It is not accurate enough to say that an interview is just a matter of two people talking to each

Chapter 9

other, but it is important to remember that it is basically just that. The purposes and roles may be different from one interview to the next, but it still comes down to our ability to talk *with* people. There are times when we're trying to get information, as in an employment interview. Sometimes we want to give information, as in an appraisal interview. It may be that we just need to listen, as we mostly do in a counseling interview. But whatever interview we are involved in, we are still using the skills of talking with people on a one to one basis. We need to learn the skills for each interview so we'll have a good idea of where we are going and when we've gotten there. We have to learn to ask questions properly, perhaps in an open-ended way or by using a reflective technique to keep the person talking. Perhaps we will have to be very direct and let the person know where he or she is missing the mark – and what the consequences are for not making the correction. These things aren't always easy and to get good at them we have to practice, study our results and practice some more.

Listening is by far the hardest part of learning how to communicate. But in an interview, listening is often the key to success. We can direct the interview by responding to whatever part of the interviewee's remark we think will lead in the right direction, but this works only if we have been listening carefully to what is being said. Bad interviews result when we fail to take our turn at *listening*. This is more than just being quiet while the other person is talking. It's a matter of listening carefully, understanding and responding appropriately. The steps in successful interviewing are simple enough to learn but take some concentration, mostly on setting our goals and then listening to see if we're getting the feedback that tells

Chapter 9

us we are going in the right direction. Once we've learned to be a good interviewer, it's surprising how much satisfaction we can get from conducting a successful interview. Since we're involved in so many interviews during our years as a manager, it's wise for us to try to get as much satisfaction as we can get.

Chapter 10

Training: The Manager's Responsibility

One of the biggest mistakes managers – new and old – make is to assume that training is a side bar to their regular job, something they only do when they have lots of time and nothing else to do. A manager who has this attitude really doesn't understand his or her job very well, since the real function of the manager is to get work done through other people. Taking this another step, we can say that our *main* job is to see that our people are trained properly. If we have anyone working for us who can't do their job because they haven't been trained, then we have failed as far as the employee is concerned.

Unless our people are properly trained, we have no justification for appraising them or for finding fault with their work. Training is a critical part of our job and we will do well to learn how to train others if we expect to succeed as managers.

Chapter 10

Training is a Skill

Unfortunately, there are many people who will treat the ability to train others as an art or science. Maybe it is, but it is a skill first and like any other skill it must be learned. Sometimes we go in the opposite direction – we tend to think of training others as something we can do with out any special skill. We may say, "What's so hard about telling someone how to do something we know all about?" The problem is, that's what we usually do and call it training – we 'tell' someone how to do it and *telling isn't training.*

There are many skills managers have to learn. We must learn to write, speak, conduct interviews and train our people. Unfortunately, we can do these things in such a way that it will make us look like we know what we are doing when we actually are not.

We watch people doing some training and it looks and sounds like they're doing a good job, but we may be fooled by what we see and hear. The people being trained may not really get the message and may go away frustrated. The people doing the training may think they have done well and go about their business thinking the employees should do their jobs properly. Later we may hear the trainers say, "Don't you remember, I told you last week how to do that?" The point is the employees get the blame for the poor job of training done by the managers. So we must learn how to train, by learning the skills of training others.

There are some things we can put off learning, but training must be learned quickly if we are to get the most

Chapter 10

work out of our people. Not only must we learn how to train quickly, but we must learn how to do it *well*. Every time we do a poor job of training someone, we waste time that can't be recovered and we get ourselves in the conflict of whether to start the training over again or to let the employee start their job not prepared and get unsatisfactory results. The truth is, we rarely repeat the training, but we do end up spending a lot of time trying to repair the damage done by poorly trained employees. The worst thing that can happen is that we end up blaming the employees for not doing their jobs properly, when we've really failed at ours.

But we can learn the basic skill of training others, if we recognize it as a skill and work hard at learning it. We cannot assume that just because we know the job we're training the employees to do, that we also know how to properly train someone on that job. Operating a drill press or creating a spreadsheet database is quite different from training someone on how to actually do the job. There are steps to training that we can identify and measure. We can tell whether or not we have done a good job and we can improve on the skill once learn what it is that makes up the skill.

Why Train

If we ask whether training is necessary, the obvious answer is, "Yes." But if we ask why we train, we get some strange answers. Some train just because there is money in the budget. Others train because the employees expect it. There are others who train because those in upper management demand it be done. Others train only when

Chapter 10

they have spare time, then they train to fill up that time. None of these are good reasons for training. Basically there are only three good reasons for training.

> The employee can't do the job.
> The employee can do it, but not well enough.
> The employee is doing the job incorrectly.

In the first case – not being able to do the job – it may be that the employees are new and have never done it before. This is an obvious case for training, but there are those who say, "Experience is the best teacher – let them learn the hard way like I did." This isn't a very practical approach for efficient work. Maybe the employees will be better able to do the job after making numerous mistakes, but who will pay for these mistakes? Who 'unlearns' the employees of all the things they have learned incorrectly. If the employees are new, then it's our job to ensure they have the opportunity to start off learning the right way to do their jobs.

Only then can we get an accurate picture of how well they're performing and progressing. But it may be that the job is new, having never been performed before by anyone in the organization. It may be a new procedure or a new piece of equipment. Here again, the employees have a right to get started on the right foot. Anytime we introduce something new, there will be enough problems without us complicating things by doing a poor job of training.

The second case – training because the employees can't do the job well enough – isn't quite as simple as the first case. It may be that the employees haven't been trained

Chapter 10

and have picked up some incorrect steps on their own. We need to speed up their production and save on wasted time. Now we are faced with the question of whether or not to train, as the employee knows something about the job already. We have to weigh the time and expense of training against the advantages of doing the job faster or better. The same is true if the employees actually had training at one point, but need more in order to better meet the standards set for our organization. We have to decide how much it's worth to get the improvement we need from better training.

Finally, there are the employees who are actually doing the job incorrectly. This is valid ground for training. How do we know the employees aren't able to do the job? We may be able to tell by the number of errors that are caused by them. It may be that by watching the employees we see that some are failing to do their jobs correctly or don't know what they are doing.

This sounds like reason enough for training, but we need to ask ourselves one basic question before we do any training; "If the employees' lives depended on it, could they do the job correctly?" If the answer to this is, "Yes", then training isn't the answer; there is some other problem and training won't solve it. So when we train, we must be sure to ask ourselves what is the reason we are training: to enable the employees to do the job; to enable them to do it better; or to enable them to do it correctly. We need to ask this question for *each* employee we train.

This all sounds simpler than it really is. If we aren't careful, we'll find ourselves training someone who has had the same training before. The employee may finish

Chapter 10

the training session and go back to the job wondering what kind of manager we are to provide training he or she has already had. Even worse, we end up giving training a bad name, because if the employee can't do the job any better after the training, some will conclude that training is a waste of time.

Another possibility for error is to train someone who isn't really going to have time to apply what he or she is learning. Maybe the employee is just a few months away from retirement or moving to another job, but because everyone else in the group had had the training, we schedule him or her for it as well. It's fine to worry about our employee's feelings, but if we send this employee for training because we don't want to hurt their feelings, we need to remember that it's also good to worry about the organization's money. How can we justify spending training money when it's obvious we can't get our money back from an employee who just won't be on the job that long.

There is another time when it is a mistake to train: when we train an employee we want to see promoted. We may train because it will look good on his or her record to have this particular training program, but not necessarily because he or she needs it. Unless this is part of the employee's regular development program, we've made a mistake in training for this reason.

The problem may come back to us in a strange way; it may get around that we have set a precedent that anyone who takes this kind of training expects to be promoted, or everyone wants to be sent to this program because they think it's the way to move up. In either case, we've put an

Chapter 10

unfair burden on the training program and asked it to do something is wasn't intended to do.

Another thing that will get us into trouble is to train someone we know hasn't got a chance to learn the job because of his or her background or lack of experience. Some managers send certain people to training programs to prove a point – that the employee is incompetent. Again, we've used training in the wrong way and have failed to do our job properly – which is to train the right people for the right reasons

Preparing to Train

Before we can do any training of our own, we must determine what it is we want to train our employees to do. This sounds simple enough, but it really isn't. For example, we should be sure we know exactly what standard of performance we are looking for. This means analyzing the job to make sure we can train someone else according to the organization's standard.

The organization has set the standard for the job itself, so we need to learn how to achieve the standards by looking at the work and not the employees who are doing the job.

Before we train, we better get any policy questions answered. We need to find out if there are any changes in the company that will make our standards wrong. If there are any acceptable deviations from the job standard, we should be aware of them before we start to train. There's no reason to avoid asking questions about standards because we can never be sure that our training has been done properly if we don't know what the standard

Chapter 10

actually is. Remember, many standards exist only because everyone has accepted them without questions. This is particularly true with things like workflow. Just because equipment or work stations got placed in a certain way doesn't mean that things flow efficiently around them.

As a result of this poor arrangement, the work has suffered, but the standard has been set. If we're not careful, we will find ourselves training to this standard. This may also be true with forms and spreadsheets. We try to train someone to fill out a complicated spreadsheet without ever questioning why it is so complex.

The truth may be that it got that way because every once in a while someone added something to it without trying to cut out anything. Pretty soon it got unwieldy but we keep on using it as the standard and keep training people to use it. A few well chosen questions might help 'un-complicate' the spreadsheet. In fact, just listening to our employees might be of some help.

They probably know that some things are unnecessary, but no one has ever bothered to ask them. Remember, they are doing the job, so no one else can be more familiar with what is actually being done than they are. If we can't come up with a better reason for doing something a certain way, we should take their word for it.

It's highly unlikely that we can ever train on everything that needs attention, so we have to decide early in the game just what it is we are going to include in the training program for each of the employees. For example, for new employees, we should concentrate on those things that

Chapter 10

will likely come up first in their new assignments. They'll have enough to do to learn the things they'll be doing immediately without worrying about things that may come up several months from now. If the job is being changed, we should concentrate on the changes, not the entire job.

It's wasteful to go through operations that the employee already understands. Even after we have decided what to do our training on, we should still check to see if there are any existing in-house programs that will do the job for us. Maybe the organization already has some kind of program that will come close enough for us to use and have us avoid developing an entire new training program.

We ask ourselves, "Why hasn't someone done this kind of training before?" Then we ask, "Who else in the organization has the same kind of training problems I do?" The answers to these questions should help us screen the organization well enough to prevent us from re-inventing the wheel.

Once we've decided on what training needs to be done and why we're doing it, we must set realistic objectives or goals for the training we are going to do. The simplest way to do this is to ask, "What do I want them to be able to do when the training is over?" Basically, the answer to this question depends on the answer to the following ones:

What actions do I want from them?

What standard do I plan to use to measure their success?

Chapter 10

What limitations or tolerances can I live with?

If we've taken a good look at the job as we suggested earlier, these things should be clear now. We should know what a satisfactory job is and if we don't, it will show up when we attempt to answer these questions. It's not enough to just say, "We want them to understand how the forming machine works." We have to specify the action and the degree of tolerance we expect to allow.

Requiring that the operator produce 100 pieces per hour with no more than two errors is much more specific than requiring that he or she understand how to use the machine. One reason, training can be so haphazard is that we go about it in a haphazard way. We just suddenly discover ourselves doing some training without much real planning. When we do a sloppy job of planning, we do a sloppy job of training. The planning doesn't have to be elaborate or time-consuming we just need to decide why the training is needed, where the training is going to take place, who will be trained and when it will be done.

Do it Right

When we train, we need to ensure we do a good job of it. As silly as that sounds, we do find that some training is better than other training – which is why some people are doing a better job than others. The reason is that we don't always know a good training job when we see one.

Managers can be heard to say, "Don't you remember, I *told* you..." which means that they think that 'telling' and 'training' are the same thing. In fact, when we watch a

Chapter 10

manager 'train' someone, they may end up doing all of the talking and doing, then leave with a statement like, "Any questions?" The employees think they understand; the operation looked simple enough, but after the manager leaves, the employees find that they can't really do the job after all.

They feel pretty stupid because they've just watched the manager do it and heard an explanation and didn't have any questions – all because the *manager* did a poor job of training. Since training is a skill, we can't expect to be good at it right away. However, we can try to learn the skill and as we do more of it, we can evaluate the results and grow with it.

Good training follows specific steps and procedures. When we train people on the job, what *we do* will have a definite bearing on how well they can perform in the future.

The most accepted process to use is a simple three step process as below:

Step 1
We tell them what to do.
We do it correctly.

Step 2
They tell us what to do.
We do it correctly.

Step 3
They tell us what to do.
They do it correctly.

Chapter 10

Note the purpose of each step. In Step 1, we tell the employees what is to be done as there will be no doubt about the action and so they will be mentally involved. Then we do it correctly, being sure they see each part of the procedure. In Step 2, they are still involved mentally as they will tell us what to do and if they tell us correctly, we do it correctly. If they are incorrect we go back to Step 1. In Step 3, they tell us what they're going to do, but not do it until we agree that they're right. If they are, then we let them do it. Step 3 can be repeated several times for practice, but it's always a good idea to keep the employees involved mentally as much as possible.

After all, this is where the memory is established. Even though we want the employees to develop good work habits, we still want them to perform with a good mental attitude. To increase this mental involvement, we can expand the three-step process to include – *what, why and how*. We still go through each step as described above, but after going through *what*, we repeat the process by telling *how*.

Then we repeat with *why* we perform the operation the way we are doing it. In other words, the first time through, we simply focus on having the employees seeing, hearing and doing the right thing.

They *see* how, but we don't go into too much detail. Then we repeat the process, this time by adding a description of *how* we do it – so that the employees hear a description of the correct way to perform the operation, while doing it. Finally, we go over the, *what* and *how* but add to it the reasons *why* we do a certain function or enter something into the computer a certain way.

Chapter 11

Leading Effective Meetings

It should be obvious that when we are doing this kind of training, we have the employees use the actual equipment that they will be using every day. If not, then we should try to find idle equipment that is similar to the kind they will be using. If they will get dirty on the job, they should get dirty during their training. If they will be entering information onto a database, they should have a database to work on during their training. There's a simple point that we miss a lot of the time: When we train, we never face the employees; we always show them from the same position they will take when they do the work. If we face them, they will see everything done backwards and may become quite confused when they try it themselves.

Classroom Training

Occasionally, managers will be asked to conduct some form of classroom training. It may be that they have

Chapter 11

become an expert in certain fields or that they have been selected to study a particular subject and then teach it within the organization. There is more to teaching a group than just having knowledge of the subject and making a good speech. The idea is to change some people's behavior on the job, which is the same reason for doing on-the-job training. We have to know what it is we want the people to be able to do; there needs to be a standard and it helps if we know the deficiencies of the people in the classroom. Once we've done this, we are ready to go into the classroom. Let's see what we need to know to make this effort successful.

There are some basic rules for classroom training that will help us understand our job better. First, people learn more by participating in the learning activity than they do by being told what they need to know. We can tell them much faster if they aren't involved, but they can forget just as fast.

Next, we should realize that the students are more likely to remember those things that they figure out themselves, than the things we figure out for them. This means that we need to let them 'discover' some of the information, themselves. This technique is called *discovery learning*.

The instructor gives the class members enough information to enable them to figure out the rest on their own. The instructor leads them along with new information, building on what they already know, then stops with a question aimed at making them think about where this is all leading. At this point, if we've done the job right, they'll get the big 'Aha' reaction and we'll have caused them to discover what it was we wanted them to learn. As a result they will remember it longer.

They will more likely to remember and learn those things most closely related to their jobs. If they are given some information or shown some new operation with the knowledge that they'll be expected to use it when they get back on the job, they'll be more likely to work at learning it. The good instructor will build in examples of on-the-job applications of these things and have a good background of stories that relate to this job function.

Obviously, not all students have the same background, not all will have the same interest in learning and not all of them have the same ability to grasp all the subjects.

This means that, *if they aren't all learning the same way, we may have to teach in different ways to reach different people.* For some, a presentation may be fine because they've always been able to grasp things quickly this way.

For others, repeating may be important, because it takes awhile for the material to soak in. Still others may require some discussion on different examples or different approaches. All of these have to be mixed into each teaching session because we can't always tell which students are learning best in which way.

However, if we pay attention only to *how* we are presenting, we will not know what the students are learning. If we get feedback from only one or two people we'll have a general idea of how well we're doing, but we won't know for sure how the class is doing until we hear

Chapter 11

all of them saying things and reacting to what we've been teaching. By simply having the class break into small groups and come up with an agreement on a certain question, it will only take a matter of minutes to find out how well we've gotten our point across. If there is much discussion and little agreement, we better start over and review. If they quickly come up with a common answer, we can reinforce this and move on.

If there are differences in the classroom, a good way to overcome them is to have the less experienced people work with the more experienced ones and the slower learners work with the quicker learners. This puts some of the responsibility on the better students and they will actually learn more by helping the others along. Most of the time, students will learn as well or better from one of their classmates than their instructor.

While we know that good teaching is more than just good public speaking. We need to make sure we understand that bad public speaking has to be overcome by even better teaching methods. We can ruin some very good instructional efforts by poor speaking efforts. Not that our students will necessarily get much more from the speaking itself if it's polished, but at least we won't detract from their learning effort if we make a good attempt at speaking well.

Follow up on Training

One final word about training: We shouldn't just train and then leave it. We should follow up on what we have done and see how well the training was understood. Training is more than doing it, marking it as completed

Chapter 11

then forgetting about it and the employees. We should go back to the employees and see how they're doing. Check their performance against the standard we set.

Check error rates, look at outputs – whatever the training was on. If the employees are performing well, we can take credit for a job well done. If not, then we need to take a look at our procedures to see if we failed to do the job properly.

The rule in this case is simple: *If the employees are doing something that we trained them on, we are responsible for their performance until we find out that something other than training is keeping them from doing their job.* Of course, we are always responsible for their performance in a way, but now we look for some other cause, because we are satisfied that the training has been done correctly.

Review

Training is the manager's responsibility. That's the heading of this chapter. It's the message within it. It's the conclusion we need to reach when we study about training. Training employees to reach their potential is a serious thing and one that can have serious consequences if not done correctly. The dangerous thing about poor training is that often it isn't the manager who gets the blame, but the poorly trained worker themselves.

Although their records show that they were trained, their performance is suffering and they will be shown as below-standard performers on those records. To make it worse, the employee may think they've been trained and give themselves a bad rating in their own minds, perhaps believing they just aren't capable of learning. To emphasize the need for good training, let's think of it this way:

It's now appraisal time. Our employees are going to be evaluated on how well they've done in their jobs over a certain period of time.

Hopefully there is a standard that is understood by both them and us as to how well they should be doing those jobs. However, we have no right to appraise them if we've failed to properly train them to that standard. Because the employees have not had the right training – 'they aren't doing their jobs up to standard.' In the appraisal, we make an entry to that effect.

How honest and fair is that? Shouldn't we make an entry that says, "Due to poor training, this employee has not yet been able to perform up to standard?" Of course, we aren't likely to make such an entry, but the employee will suffer from the poor appraisal for a long period of time. It may even be a part of their permanent record and all because we didn't do our job very well.

On the other hand, think about it from a standpoint of having done a good job. It's now appraisal time and our employees are doing their jobs up to standard. Even though we aren't likely to say that they are doing so well as a result of our training, we can take satisfaction of knowing that when we did our job properly our employees responded with good performances and that, too, will be on their records for a long time.

We can be pleased with this kind of result, especially if we get it frequently. And we should if we learn our training skills well.

Chapter 11

Meetings are a way of life and can be an important thread throughout most organizations. However, the reason we may tend to think negatively of them is that they can take up a lot of our time when we don't have time to spare.

One of the main reasons we may feel negatively about meetings is that we may have never experienced the satisfaction of attending a well run meeting, one that accomplishes specific goals quickly and efficiently and ends when the purpose has been met. The purpose of this book is to establish the basis of conducting meetings with these goals in mind.

To start we need to consider the following eleven questions:

What is the purpose of the meeting?
What is the expected product?
Who should attend?
When should they be notified?
How should they be notified?
Are some people more important to the meeting than others?
If seating arrangement is important, where will everyone sit?
Can we assign certain leadership roles to some people – if so, who?
What time is the meeting scheduled to start?
What time is the meeting scheduled to end?
How much flexibility do we have?

Chapter 11

Preparation

Without proper planning and control, meetings can run poorly and accomplish very little. If meetings are run properly, they can accomplish things that cannot be done in any other way. The first thing we need to accept is that meetings need a precise purpose. Meetings are necessary and we should approach them with a positive attitude. We should also approach them with an idea of knowing what the particular *purpose* of the meeting is.

Is the purpose a problem-solving meeting?

Have problems arisen that we need to meet and discuss as a group? If so, then we must approach the meeting with the information needed for problem-solving. We need to set it up as follows:

Define the problem
Gather appropriate information
Find the cause
Find alternative solutions
Pick a solution
Put the plan to work
Carry out the plan
Follow up on the solution

Is the purpose a decision making meeting?

We need to remember that nobody should leave the meeting without knowing exactly what the final decision was. We need to ensure that whoever is appointed to carry out the decision is clear and well prepared upon leaving the meeting. If we are leading this meeting it is our responsibility to follow up to ensure that the decision was implemented correctly.

Is the purpose a brainstorming meeting?

Has someone decided that the best way to reach a solution or develop an idea or attack a problem is to have a group of people get together and do some brainstorming? If so, then we must be sure that we understand the process. Will we discipline ourselves to avoid letting any negative thinking enter the session? Since we are conducting the meeting, it is our responsibility to ensure that everything goes well.

Is the purpose for attitude development?

It may be that the meeting is to be a "pep rally", aimed at increasing loyalty or improving sales. Maybe there is a quality control problem and this meeting is for the purpose of changing attitudes towards this matter. If so, we need to know it and aim it in that direction. Even if the meeting is just for the purpose of educating our group on new policy or product or services, we should settle this in our minds and build our planning around it.

The point is that if we are going to run the meeting, we need to know its specific purpose. After all, we are asking a number of people to give up their work time to come to our meeting. They have a right to expect that we know the

Chapter 11

real objective of the meeting and what we are trying to accomplish.

As a meeting leader, we need to ask ourselves, "What *specific activities* will take place?" This is important in the arrangement of furniture, having the proper equipment, the selection of the room, etc... The activities will determine whether we will need to seat everyone in a circle or with all chairs facing the front or what table configurations we will need. Thinking of these things in advance will make us look good and will definitely help make the meeting a success. But we need to know more.

We should decide on the *specific timing* for the meeting – not just how long it will run, but when will we have it. What day? What time of day? If it's to be a one hour meeting, why run it at a time that will conflict with an established morning or afternoon break? Alternatively, if it's to be a lengthy one, providing for a break in the middle might be a good way to inject some relief. Having meetings at the end of the day or end of the week, when people are tired and thinking about going home, might not be the best time to schedule a brainstorming session.

If we aren't sure how long the meeting will take, running it too close to lunch or the end of the day may get us into trouble. What happens if we need more time? Usually when time runs out and we don't want to call another meeting, we begin to make hurried decisions and leave some things hanging in limbo. When the meeting is over and we review the results, we may discover that some important things got overlooked, or that some of the things we decided may not be very practical after all.

Chapter 11

Finally, on specifics, the meeting leader needs to know the *specific attendance*. Not just how many are to attend, but who. There is always the consideration of seating, both as to who sits where and how many seats will be required. If the leader has any control over the selection of those to attend, we need to go back and look at the objective of the meeting. If this is to be an educational meeting, then maybe more people in attendance will be better.

On the other hand, if there is to be problem-solving or decision making, the number needs to be held to a minimum. The basic requirement for a smaller meeting is to have enough people there to represent everybody concerned, but not to weight it with too many people from one side of the argument or from one department.

Meeting attendees do not want to be put in a position where they may be up against a stacked room. They have just as much right to their opinion as others, but if the 'other side' brought along more than their share of representatives, then things are *unequal*. The way to avoid this is to look at the list of suggested attendees and decide whether there is fair representation from all departments, groups, etc... If not, then a private suggestion to the appropriate people may be the best way to solve the problem.

These things make a big difference in the outcome of a successful meeting and meeting leaders should do whatever is necessary to control the attendance and the particular people attending.

Chapter 11

Physical Facilities

Of all the things that can make or break a meeting, perhaps nothing can have more influence than the place where the meeting is held and the equipment that is being used. No matter how well the leader coordinates the timing and the speaking and the interchange of ideas and movement of information, if the room is poorly ventilated, or too hot or too cold, all of this will go to accomplish very little. Actually, setting up the facilities isn't difficult when we consider the some basic elements. We can divide the problem areas as follows:

Creature comforts
Acoustics
Visibility
Interference

Let's look at them individually. First, the *creature comforts* – those things that affect our senses, starting with the ventilation we have already mentioned. Is there a means of regulating the ventilation or temperature quickly if the room gets too hot or too cold? We want to be sure we have control of the facility as far as the temperature is concerned.

Many other things affect our comfort, some of which may seem insignificant. For example, we can sit in a molded plastic chair and it will feel comfortable. But after a short time it becomes very uncomfortable, because it was molded for one position – and we do not sit in one position for very long. Many people find it difficult to remain comfortable in chairs that do not have arms. If there is a table to lean on it's not too bad, but if not, when

Chapter 11

they try to relax or lean back, their arms will drop to their sides in an uncomfortable way. Also, if the table is too high or too low in relation to the chairs, the attendees will feel themselves straining to get comfortable. Remember too, that there is such a thing as being *over-comfortable*. If the meeting is likely to produce a few periods of boredom, soft easy chairs will not add to the alertness of the group.

The matter of *acoustics* is of obvious importance, but there are some problems that may not be apparent from just looking at a facility. For example, sound carries better in an empty room than in a full one. Even if a room appears to carry our voice very well, we still need to know what it will sound like when there are several people in the room.

One way to check this is to have someone stand at one end of the room with us at the other end and have them talk in a low voice. Not in a whisper, but in a conversational tone, as if they were talking to someone next to them, because often, that's what people do in meetings – they talk as though they were taking to the person next to them. If we can hear without any trouble, we can be assured that things will be heard when the room is full.

Visibility is always a problem and one that can cause good meetings to go sideways. If the meeting is to be built around charts, videos or other visuals and some people will not be able to see, then obviously they won't get much out of the meeting. But, that's not the only problem Even if people are to be seated at a table and no visuals are to be used, they still like to be able to see the speaker.

Chapter 11

This should be considered when the chairs are arranged, or the tables set out. Many meetings are ruined because all of the people are aligned along two sides of a table. Each time someone says something, everybody leans over to see what is happening. Each has to lean out farther than the last and pretty soon some are saying to themselves, "What's the use?"

Interference at a key point in a meeting can cause a near disaster, especially if we have spent valuable time building up our case. Just about the time we are making our point, hoping for agreement with the group, the caterer arrives with fresh coffee and muffins. We, along with the group are distracted and we may need to start over on some points. We need to pre-determine what time any food and beverage service may be coming into the room.

This may seem obvious, but we can avoid most interference with a little planning and coordinating. There is another kind of interference that is much more subtle. There are the participants who may check and respond to text message and emails during the meeting.

While they may be trying to be efficient, they are interrupting the meeting and are hurting the chances of a successful meeting.

An instruction at the start of the meeting to turn off all personal devices will help a lot, but also add when we will be taking breaks to allow for message checking will be a much better guarantee.

Chapter 11

Conducting the Meeting

Interestingly enough, our role as meeting leader may vary from meeting to meeting and even during any particular meeting. This is why it is so important to know exactly what the purpose of the meeting is. If we know this, then we can more easily tell what our role is.

Primarily, our function is to see that someone takes all of the roles required to run a good meeting, which may mean that we will have to assume those not taken by others.

If we are in charge of the meeting, the best thing we can do is to assign roles effectively to others. We can put someone in charge of the 'initiating' role, someone else in the 'timekeeping' role and some else in the 'minute taking' role, etc... This way we can keep up with what is going on and know when to step in and take over a role not being taken by someone else.

The thing to remember is that good leaders aren't necessarily seen and heard all of the time. Effective leaders simply see that everything runs smoothly, regardless of who is seen and heard the most. Most often we mistake the word 'leader' to mean the person standing in the front of the room, the one giving direction or the one moving the meeting on to the next point.

This may be us, or it may be someone we have assigned to the role because we know they have a suitable ability at that particular function.

Chapter 11

Hidden Agendas

One interesting and frustrating thing about many meetings is that there often exists, undercurrents of thoughts, needs, ideas and objectives that never quite get out into the open. These things have been called *hidden agendas*. Hidden agendas are simply those objectives that people bring to meetings that may differ from the real purpose of the meeting.

Even though the stated purpose may be to discuss staff overtime, we may really want to say a few things about work standards and may even want to get some answers on the subject.

As decisions are being made, we may appear to be basing our suggestions on common sense or the needs of the group, but we may have a hidden agenda that tells us that certain things would be more popular with the boss or make our department look better.

It is difficult to pinpoint every hidden agenda that is brought to the meeting by each member of the group, but at least we should be aware that there will definitely be some there. We should also be aware that they can affect the meeting results because they tend to produce biased answers.

The first time we get an answer that surprises us because it doesn't sound reasonable in terms of the discussion so far, we might want to consider that a hidden agenda is at work. We should ask ourselves, "What else could make John say that? Has he said something else before that indicates that there may be pressure from within his

Chapter 11

department? Is he trying to protect his job, his people or his boss?" The interesting thing is that we won't necessarily take any action on John's hidden agenda, but we'll be sure to consider what he says in terms of what his needs are.

The main thing is not to try to become a mind reader during the meeting. There may be a need to address these items with John outside of the meeting at another time.

We may never know exactly why people react the way they do – they may not even know, but if we see them beginning to fit a pattern, we should be alert enough to understand what they're doing and why.

If we feel certain that we know what's causing someone to react a certain way, we can use this to our advantage.

If we think that someone has a hidden agenda that will cause them to be very budget conscious, we can direct our attention towards that person with ideas about saving money and even draw them out on these particular items.

On the other hand, we may try to avoid getting such a person involved in matters that deal with cost increases.

Feedback

One of the things that tell us that hidden agenda exists in our group is the kind of feedback we get from our participants. Without the proper amount of feedback, we can't tell how the group feels, what individuals are thinking, what direction we should take or how well we are doing at directing the meeting towards its goal. While

Chapter 11

it's obvious *why* we need feedback, it isn't always obvious *how* we get it. Let's look at some ways of getting feedback, remembering that the purpose is to use the information toward controlling the meeting and reaching the objectives we have set.

If the group is small, it isn't too difficult to get the feedback. Usually a small group means less formality with everyone saying what they think and it isn't hard to get the participants to answer a question directed to them and they may even volunteer to give their opinions. As the size of the group increases, the problems of getting feedback increase.

Now we have to use some techniques that will encourage the participants to give us the feedback we need. For example, we can simply go around the room and ask for comments on specific subjects.

We can ask for a show of hands for both agreement and disagreement. We need to be careful though as there will always be people who disagree but do not put up their hand.

In this case we watch and see who doesn't hold up their hand for either response and then ask them how they feel. If nothing else happens, it will get them in the habit of responding one way or another in the future.

Since people coming to the meeting are supposed to represent certain viewpoints, they aren't doing their job properly if they don't express themselves. We may have to help them along by asking direct questions, not to embarrass them but to get their input as they have been

Chapter 11

invited to share their knowledge. We can ask a question such as, "We haven't heard from you Susan. What do you think about this issue?"

Another technique we can use is to have the participants talk in small groups and then report to the whole group. This way they smooth over their differences in the small sessions and not in front of the entire group.

Often people just want to be sure that they have had a chance to be heard and they are just as satisfied to do it before a small group than a larger group.

The leader can ensure that good ideas get out to the entire group by listening to the smaller sub groups and then when the larger group re-forms, giving one member a cue to bring out a point that we feel will bring out the point we are trying to make. Such as, "Didn't I hear you saying that this wasn't really a problem in your office anymore?" We need to be careful that we aren't suggesting that we already know what we want them to say and that if they don't say it, we'll do it for them. Nothing will kill their incentive any quicker.

What do we do with this feedback once we have gotten it? We use it to direct and control the meeting. We see how far along the participants are and if they aren't doing as well as we think they should be, we need to take steps to move things along faster.

If they are on schedule, we make note of it and keep them on the same track. If they seem to be ahead of where we thought they would be, we may even consider concluding

Chapter 11

the meeting early or plan to undertake additional items in the meeting.

But this isn't the only function of the feedback. If we hear someone say something that is important and we want to reinforce it to the group, we can say something like, "How about going over that again Ron.

That is the best way I've heard it put so far." Another use for feedback is to give us something to use to help us get to the next topic with. When we have exhausted a subject and feel it's time to move on, the ideal way is to do it by using some of the feedback: "Okay, Bridgette, that really takes us to the next subject, doesn't it? The way you have expressed it is...."

The transition is smooth and we don't appear to be completely dominating the session. Bridgette gets credit for "initiating" something new, the group gets an introduction to what is going to be talked about and we know things are running smoothly.

Conflict

We need to understand and expect to run into some conflict during our meetings. Our first reaction when we meet conflict in our meeting is to become a little unnerved. We think conflict is bad and will ruin our carefully planned out meeting. Of course, too much conflict *can* ruin a meeting, but a certain amount should be expected and planned for.

Chapter 11

We've already seen that people have hidden agendas, so we shouldn't think that the meeting alone has caused the conflict. Also, when people feel strongly enough about something that may cause conflict among themselves and others, that means they are involved and have some commitment on the subject being discussed. We should be glad this is the case and try our best to use it our advantage.

First we need to be sure to recognize conflict when it surfaces in the meeting. Snide remarks, digs at other participants and other obvious signs aren't hard to recognize as signs of conflicts. More subtle signs are withdrawals, over-politeness, too quick committal and frequent efforts to go back and discuss topics that have been already closed.

There is no reason to ever to let conflict break out into open hostility such as name-calling, shouting, etc... We keep this from happening by stepping in before things get this far. The best thing to do is to use this to our advantage by formalizing the debate, thus relieving some of the steam, or by trying to state the conclusions of each side, thereby directing the attention away from the disagreeing participants and back to us.

By restating the positions and possibly throwing in more facts, we can often resolve the conflict. But, *we may not want to resolve it too quickly*. With conflict we have involvement, interest and participation. Without conflict, we may not have any of these things.

When there is conflict, at least we know people are giving us their opinions. We also see others taking sides, thus

Chapter 11

committing themselves. We are, in a way, getting some of the best feedback we could hope for. As long as it is productive, let's keep it going! When we feel it has done all the good it can do and may be starting to do some harm, we need to step in and put a stop to it.

We can do this in the following ways: taking a stand ourselves and asking for a commitment from all concerned, or by gradually working our way into the conversation and turn it around to more productive topics.

Another way, which is not the best, but may be necessary, is to simply point out that while the situation is interesting, it probably isn't getting us very far. If conflict persists, we may have to postpone that portion of the meeting to a later date. Most often, the group as a whole will put enough pressure on the individuals so that the situation will work itself out and there should not be a need for another meeting.

Using the participants

Most people who are good at conducting meetings or conferences have learned a simple skill: they use the other participants to help make the meeting a good one. *They share the leadership roles.*

They recognize that it takes more than one person in a meeting to get the job done, so they don't just allow group members to assume various roles; they *plan* to get them into those roles.

Chapter 11

They've learned for example, that if somebody else does a good job of summarizing, let them do it. If somebody is conscious of the time and reminds the group about deadlines, the leader thanks the person for reminding them of the time factor and doesn't resent it. If somebody plays the "devil's advocate, " asking questions and taking the opposite side to test the ideas being discussed, the leader will let them do it because they need that role played and it's best played by one of the participants. Good leaders know that when people participate in a meeting and think of it as their own, they'll be much more likely to support the results that come out of it.

To best understand this, we have to remember the last meeting we were at when the leader played all of the roles. The leader kept us on track; the leader reminded us of the time; the leader interrupted the long winded participant; the leader praised good ideas and questioned bad ones.

The leader asked, "Will people really support that idea?" The leader negotiated compromise among the various positions and thoughts; the leader introduced new ideas when things began to wind down too soon; the leader brought out those who weren't talking or contributing. When we watch such a person, we might think that they are doing such a wonderful job. We might even think of patterning ourselves after this leader, thinking how nice it was to have everything under control.

So what is wrong with this approach to leading meetings? The problem is simple: It was never anybody's meeting but the leader's. Everyone sat back and was content with a *what do you want me to do now?* mentality. They

Chapter 11

contributed only when they were told to and stopped when told to. They were supporting the leader and not the reason for the meeting. It never became the participant's meeting therefore the end product is not theirs either.

Successful meetings are the result of smart leaders sharing the meeting *and* the purpose with the other participants. They begin the planning with this in mind and never let up. It's always, *our* meeting. It's always, *we* need to solve this problem. When people arrive for the meeting, each should be greeted as a special person bringing ideas and solutions and the ability to tackle the problems presented.

If someone has something special to report, their names are on the agenda and we mention their name at the start of the meeting to give them the proper recognition. Roles may even be assigned – such as someone to take notes and someone to serve as time keeper – to people who are willing to play those roles. The effective leader will observe people falling into certain roles and let them do so. If someone seems good at sensing the need for compromise and starts working towards that, they should be allowed to continue without interruption. The leader will take a mental note of this and will call on this person later if it seems a compromise needs to be worked out.

The next time any of us attends a meeting, watch and see if the roles are being shared. It's entirely possible that a good meeting can run for its duration with the leader sitting back, observing and doing very little. The best thing for us is to try it ourselves. If we've been designated as the leader, we take it gladly, but before or during the

Chapter 11

meeting see if we can get others to play the roles we've talked about.

Leadership Roles

We've talked a lot about the leadership roles people play. Here's a brief summary of these roles and the part each plays. Think about them the next time a meeting comes along and see if anybody but the leader is playing them. We can also play some of them ourselves in support of the leader.

Harmonizer: Keeps the atmosphere friction free; looks for points of agreement rather than stirring disagreement. Will recognize supporting statements from different participants and bring them out.

Compromiser: Will work for agreement by using trade-offs. Recognizes when people are willing to give in on certain points and which things they feel strongly about. Serves as a moderator in negotiation.

Conscience: Reminds the group of the goal and makes efforts to keep them moving. May single people out to move toward the goal. Expresses discomfort when group is needlessly hung up on an unimportant point.

Gatekeeper: Understands the process of moving a group off-center. Will use techniques of questioning, repetition or reflection to get things going. Knows when the group is ready to move to another point.

Catalyst: Asks creative and even uncomfortable questions to get the group thinking. Will be able to bring in quieter participants by arousing emotions or getting them involved in one of the issues.

Summarizer: Keeps group aware of where they are. Marks their progress with a summary or feedback on decisions. Recognizes when there is repetition or discussion on topics already covered and moves the group on with a good transition statement. May take notes for group or even work on the white board to summarize.

Ending the Meeting

Just as it is important to know how to plan, start and conduct a meeting, it is important to know how and when to end one. Why should this be a problem? Isn't everyone anxious to leave the meeting and go back to their work? Yes, probably so, but that's the problem; we let them go before we have taken care of some important matters. For example, when it appears we have covered all of the necessary points and reached a proper conclusion – does the group know what the conclusions are? Do the people know what we have agreed to do and say? Do they know who's supposed to do what? These things have to be

Chapter 11

taken care of or else all of our efforts will be wasted. Maybe just a summary statement is all that is needed. "So this is what we've agreed to do: First we will tell..." By stating these things clearly and concisely, we are asking for commitment and consent.

If we have watched the meeting closely, there shouldn't be any misunderstandings. But we state the agreements anyway, so there will be no doubts. But we also state the action we have planned and who has the responsibility for taking care of the action. We make sure all participants understand their roles and are committed to carrying them out. If another meeting is required or some reporting period is necessary, this should be settled without doubt. If certain people are to finish certain actions before the next meeting, a schedule should be worked out and the timetable agreed to. If we suspect that one or more of the people don't really know what they're supposed to do, or aren't committed, this is the time to get it straight. Once the meeting is over, it's going to be difficult to take care of things.

Following Up On the Meeting

It would seem that after all that has been done so far to make this a successful meeting, there can't possibly be anything left to do. Maybe not, but don't be too sure. There at least three things that need to be done before we can call it a completely successful meeting. First, we need to check on the action of the people who had things to do and deadlines to meet. Are they staying on schedule? Are they doing what the meeting group really decided on?

Chapter 11

Have they run into problems that were not anticipated? We need to ask these questions and find the answers.

Secondly, we should report the outcome of the meeting to those who need to be advised. The report does not need to be a long list of notes or the entire minutes of the meeting, but should contain enough information so that those who could not attend or will be affected by the result, will know what was done and what was planned.

Finally, we need to take a look at the meeting as an effort to improve our own ability to lead effective meetings. How did we do? Were there things that should have been handled differently? Will we make the same mistakes again, or do we see where we went wrong? Did we handle the conflict well? Did we recognize the support we were getting from some of the participants and did we make use of it?

As we learn, we will make mistakes, however, if we don't look at our actions and our mistakes with the goal of doing better the next time, our next mistakes are our own fault.

Review

Good meetings aren't measured by how well we handled the participants or how close we came to the proposed finishing time – but by the results. How we handled the meeting will have some effect on the results, but there is a lot more to it than that. Results will depend on how well the meeting was planned, how well we did in selecting the participants, how well they understood and played their

Chapter 11

roles in the meeting and how well we did in sharing the various functions of leading the meeting. If we ended up playing all the roles, from gatekeeper to summarizer, we may have had a good meeting, but it's doubtful that anyone else did.

We select some people to come together to meet because a problem exists and they are the people who are concerned with the problem or who have some information that will help in solving that problem. Our job as meeting leader is to use those people in such a way that there won't be a problem after we've had the meeting or after we carry out the action decided on, by the people attending. This means that we use these resources to do what they can do best: solve the problem at hand. If further action is required we make sure to get their commitment to the solution by involving them both in the strategy of problem-solving and the necessary action.

We should never leave a meeting without all participants knowing exactly what is expected of them and when they are to complete what they have agreed to do. Finally, it is important that there be the follow up we mentioned. See to it that they do their part. That's *our* part.

Chapter 12

Problem-Solving

Problem-solving, like most other things discussed so far, is a skill. There are specific steps in the process which, when properly followed, should guarantee success. The difficulty often comes when we start to look at the process, because the steps sound complicated. Actually, the process is simple and is the one we use most of the time in our personal decisions. When we consider buying a car, a house, or a boat, we go through these steps. We don't necessarily go through them consciously, but we still use them. As we discuss the steps, it's a good idea to think about how we use them in solving our everyday problems. Even though we use the steps in our personal decisions, there seems to be some reason why we don't always use the application in our jobs. For example, we realize that when we buy things we may need to use our credit cards and in the process could end up paying additional charges in interest payments – but we fail to see that the organization we work for can run into the same problem. We will look at the steps, see how they

Chapter 12

work, give some examples and leave it up to the manager to make the application on his or her own. The steps may sound complicated, but they really aren't that hard to understand and apply.

Defining the Problem

The first step in problem-solving is to be sure we are attacking the *right* problem. An employee comes to us and claims to be tired of working on a certain job. If we take that at face value and start to solve the problem, we may find that we are the wrong problem and may be creating another. In reality, the employee may be fed up with us as a manager, or have issues with a co-worker or be making more mistakes than necessary because he or she hasn't had enough training.

How do we know whether we are trying to solve the right problem? The best way is to do what a doctor does when examining a patient – get all the symptoms together and see what kind of picture develops. This way we won't be treating just a symptom, but the real problem. Once we identify the symptoms we start to ask "What are the things that could produce these symptoms?" If employees are doing poor work, that may be a symptom of poor supervision or poor working conditions. Are there other signs, such as high turnover rates, absenteeism, lateness, etc.? Are some of the employees performing fine while others are not? Have these same employees performed better in the past? Only after we have satisfied ourselves with the answers to these questions can we be sure we are solving the correct problem and not just treating a symptom. Once we are sure we know what the problem is, it's a good idea to state it for our own clarification.

Chapter 12

"Reduce loss of production time. Reduce the error rate. Increase the overall production rate for the group." Note that it's not the time to say, "Reduce the error rate caused by union intervention." This assumes that we already know the cause of the problem, which may be the case, but it's a good idea to get a few more facts before stating this. This brings us to the next step in the problem-solving process.

Gathering Information

The information stage is an important one, but one that's often taken too lightly. After all, we've spent all this time defining the problem, haven't we got enough information? No, not at this stage, we aren't ready to solve the problem yet. We just want to get as much information as we can to help us be sure we really are solving the right problem. Once we've gathered as many facts as possible, we take one last look and see if we really are on the right track. Have we discovered that every manager before us has had the same problem with the same employees on the same job? This doesn't make the problem go away, but it does change the complexion of the problem.

One of the important decisions that managers must be able to make is to know when to stop looking and start solving. We must recognize that to go any further would take more time and effort than the problem deserves. All information should be gathered with an open mind. It would be improper to gather only that information that will help us prove a point, rather than solve the real problem. If we go into the problem-solving process with

Chapter 12

preconceived notions then following specific procedures is just a useless exercise.

It is essential during this information gathering stage, that we get specific information, rather than generalities. We need to find out things like who or what, how many, how much, where, when, how long, etc.

We will find that this kind of information is harder to get than general comments, but much more reliable in the long run. For example, it's not enough to have statements like, "She's late all the time." We need to ask, "How many times in the last month?" We shouldn't accept information like, "This machine is costing us a fortune in repair bills."

We need to ask, "How much is a fortune?" Generalities and opinions are much easier to get and we probably make more friends when we ask their opinions instead of making them dig up *specific* information. But we are trying to solve a *specific* problem and hopefully recommend that *specific* action be taken.

If all of this is based on only opinions, then we aren't likely to have the best solution available. If some information is questionable, we should note it, because otherwise we may find ourselves making decisions on that information as if it were completely reliable.

If we know that there is some doubt as to the validity of the information, we'll treat it with caution later on. If not, we may forget and create problems for ourselves that could easily have been avoided.

Chapter 12

Finding the Cause

The reason we have stressed the fact that we aren't yet ready for the solution is that at this point we are only ready to identify the *cause* of the problem. Only when we have found the cause can we select an appropriate solution. Using the information we have gathered, we look at all possible causes. If we decide that the cause of the poor work output is the result of inadequate training, not poor work habits, then we have some valuable data to use toward applying the proper solution.

The difficult thing to remember is that causes aren't always easy to find. Rather than say that the cause is not obvious, we should say that the cause that is obvious may not be the real problem.

If we have a problem because one of the workers in the office is being rude with people in other departments, the cause may not be his or her bad attitude; it may be that we haven't made the assignment completely clear and the worker is protecting his or her job in what seems to be the safest way – by keeping others away from it. "I'm sorry, but I'm too busy to help you." Or "Did the boss tell you to do that?" or "That's my job and I don't want you messing it up."

The cause may be poor supervision, poor definition of work responsibility, inadequate training or several other things. But if we've gotten enough information, we should have a pretty good idea at this stage what the real cause of the problem is.

Chapter 12

After we are sure we have the cause isolated, it's still a good idea to take a quick check of past history. Did this same thing cause the same problem before? Has this same problem been caused by a shift change or a new piece of equipment? There are a couple good reasons for checking past history when we have identified the cause.

First, has someone identified this as a cause before and tried to solve the problem by eliminating the cause? Did the problem go away? Did it turn out to be only part of the solution? Are the basic ingredients still there – the same people, the same office, the same equipment? If they are did the solution just fail to take effect or has something else – some new ingredient entered into the picture?

The second good reason for checking history is to find out if there is any record of the problem going away *by itself.* Some problems are that way. When there is a change in the office routine, trouble develops. We know that we should do something but aren't sure just what.

Then before we know it, the problem has disappeared. The danger in this kind of thinking is that most of us tend to expect that *all* problems will go away sooner or later. Many potentially good managers have failed by waiting for the problems to disappear.

Even many problems that seem to leave, come back in another form – often much worse. So we can't wait just because some problems do go away. But we can find out if this particular thing has a history of repeating itself, then going away. For example, when it's time to replace a laptop in the office, we can be sure that there will be

Chapter 12

someone who isn't happy with your selection of the person who gets it, no matter how fair it is. A check with managers who have been around for awhile will tell us that it's alright – this will wear off by itself. If we are satisfied that this is right, and the new laptop caused the problem, then we can be equally satisfied that time will heal the problem just as well as any other solution we may have picked.

Finding Alternative Solutions

Now comes the tricky stage where we have already determined the cause and are going to try to find the best solution, the solution that will eliminate whatever is causing the problem. The reason this is tricky is that it is the last time we can really use much imagination or ingenuity. What we want to do now is to think of several possible solutions, not just one.

We want the best one and there is a way of getting it. The process is to brainstorm and think of as many alternatives or options as possible without making any efforts to evaluate them or decide on one, or throw any of them out. The most important thing is that we must not allow ourselves to think, "I'm sure that won't work, so I'll rule it out now." About the only rule is to concentrate on those solutions that will most likely remove the cause we have located. If there is doubt, *keep the idea around anyway*, it can lead to other ideas.

The problem with evaluating too early is that we may overlook some good ideas by just not getting around to thinking about them. We may quickly hit on an idea that

Chapter 12

sounds good and go with it, but we never thought about the alternatives that may have been better in the long run. To make it worse, the idea we picked to solve our problem may end up being less effective than we hoped, either because it had flaws in it or it wasn't as practical as it sounded in the beginning. By the time we find out, we may find ourselves committed to this and have to support it knowing it isn't the best solution to our problem.

After we have spent some time listing all the ideas that we can think of, we should take a last look at them and see if anything else comes to mind. This will tell us if we've paid too much attention to just a single line of thought. Often ideas cause us to think of other ideas, so the time may be well spent. We also need to look at the problem and decide how much time its worth. The bigger the problem, the more time can be committed to solving it. We can spend too much time looking for alternatives – where we reach a point when the same amount of time no longer produces the same quality of alternative.

An advantage of listing the options we have looked at is that at some point we can say, "I considered these other options but here is why I chose this one." If we have done a good job of thinking out our decisions, we can show why the way we took is better than the ones we rejected. If for some reason there is a need to take one of the other options due to company policy, budget considerations, etc. then it's also good to be able to say, "I considered that also and if we go that route, then here are the things that will have to be done..." A final advantage is that it's sometimes possible to sell an idea by showing what the alternatives are. If someone doesn't like what we have chosen, it's good to be able to provide alternatives.

Chapter 12

Picking a Solution

Now that we've gone through all of this, how do we pick the best solution from the options we have listed. There are some definite steps we need to consider. It would be a shame to go this far in such a careful manner and then lose all of the advantage by not using the same careful approach in picking the best alternative. The approach should be a screening process to look at each of the options we have picked and see if they meet certain criteria. If so, then we can use them; if not, then we can eliminate them one by one.

We ask ourselves if the alternative we are looking for is really *possible*. We said earlier that we didn't want to rule out any ideas at that point, but now we can be very critical. Now is the time when we decide whether or not the idea will really work. Is it within the capability of our group, our talents, our budget? Next, we ask ourselves if the alternative is really *workable*. Even if we have the capabilities, will it really work under the conditions that exist in our work situation?

Will our people accept the idea? Will this option fit into our way of doing things, considering the routine, our interfacing with other work groups? Then we ask ourselves whether the alternative we are considering is really a *probable* solution. What is the *probability* that the idea will work and will be used? Is the idea *applicable* to this problem at this time under these circumstances?

This last question is the most critical of all. We must be sure that the solution applies to the real problem. As we study the alternative to see whether or not to use it, we want to know not only whether or not it applies to the specific problem, but whether it solves *all* of it? We should be comfortable with an alternative if we are sure that it fits the problem and will solve all of it. Once we have chosen an alternative, we need to *state it very clearly.* We should make sure that everyone who learns about the solution knows exactly *who is going to do what* and what it will take in terms of people, money and time.

If we have decided to move certain people to new locations, we should specify which people, where they will go and what will be their job responsibilities when they get there. If we have decided to go into overtime, we should state how much overtime will be required, who will work it and how much it will cost. Once the people involved have been told, the information can be reinforced in a group email and we should make time to be available if someone has questions or concerns.

Putting the Plan to Work

How do we go about introducing a new idea? We have to ask certain questions, we have to anticipate problems and try to decide ahead of time how we will handle them. For example, we should ask ourselves, "Who will likely resist this solution?" If we anticipate that one of the older workers will try to kill the idea, we should take steps to prevent this, even if this means going to the worker and getting him or her to help introduce it or give us some suggestions on ways to make it work. We need to decide what risks are involved in trying this new or different idea and who will likely misunderstand what we are trying to do. Is our boss in agreement? Will he or she back us up

Chapter 12

when questions arise or opposition appears? After we've tried to anticipate who will be affected and what problems this will cause, we should see whether all risks, resistance and resentments are covered. If so, it's time to carry out the plan we've chosen. Going through these steps should give us the confidence to go ahead with the solution to the problem.

Executing the Plan

Now comes the important part of making our plan operate. We have spent valuable time arriving at what we think is the best solution to the problem. We have confidence that it is going to work, but it won't work by itself. If the plan is not executed the way we've specified, the results will make the solution *look* like the wrong one, even if it's not. The solution deserves as much careful attention in the work stage as it did in the selection stage.

Executing the plan means more than just putting it to work, or telling someone else to do the job. It means keeping track of the progress, watching how well things are going, even making adjustments along the way. We must be careful to avoid being so committed to the plan that we can't see things that are going wrong. Our commitment is to the *job*, not our plan. This doesn't mean that we have to sit around watching everything that happens. If we have confidence in the plan, we should be able to let it run its course.

Occasional spot checking should tell us if we are really solving the problem. If we have reassigned some of the workers to different jobs, then we can assess by reviewing production numbers on a sampling basis. If the sales

Chapter 12

territory has been changed, the occasionally checking of the current results with previous ones will tell us everything we should need to know.

While, we are watching the plan in operation it's a good idea to be aware of any potential trouble. We've already talked about making a note on where we might expect opposition or misunderstanding. Since we know this ahead of time, we have some good check points. The key is to know when trouble is brewing so we can head it off not wait until things are in bad enough shape to step in.

The skill of anticipating trouble is a hard but valuable one to learn. Most trouble can be stopped easily when it first starts than after it's gone on for awhile. If we suspect that someone is going to misunderstand or not like the plan we are implementing, we better make sure that they don't form too many opinions before we deal with their misunderstandings. It will be a lot harder to change their minds than if help them to make up their minds in the first place.

Part of the reason for watching the progress of our solution is to check on our own problem-solving ability. We will need to know how well we did at defining the problem, selecting the alternatives and picking the right option. Not only will we want to know how well we did at this, but will want to get a look at the value of the solution. As we think about our future problem-solving efforts, we will want to ask ourselves, "Was all of this done efficiently, or did I spend too much time coming up with a solution?" "Did I do a poor job of anticipating where the trouble would come from?" All of this leads us to the final step – following up on the solution after the plan has been put to work.

Following Up on the Solution

The simple question we ask now is, "Did the solution work?" The answer will tell us what we want to know. No matter how thoroughly we planned or how well we implemented it, if it didn't solve the problem, it really wasn't very good. But if it worked and we got the benefits we thought we would, then we would have to say the solution was a good one. If possible, we should try to find out *why* the solution worked.

This may seem strange, but there is always the possibility that the problem disappeared in spite of what we did. This means that we try to determine whether other factors contributed at the same time which may have had an effect on the outcome of our problem-solving effort. While this isn't worth a lot of time, it's still worth looking at to keep us from getting caught thinking that we have solved a problem by ourselves when really some other factors may have solved it.

We should always be looking for flaws in the solution. How might we have avoided the negative things that happened? Were there obvious signs that we missed or was the error unavoidable? Would it have been worth the extra time to look longer for possible trouble? This is hindsight, but it's valuable. It can help us avoid making the same mistakes again. It can help us measure our own ability at problem-solving. It can be of help to future problem solvers, because if we have a good idea of what

Chapter 12

happened, they can learn from both our successes and failures. Of course, all of this assumes that the problem is dead and not just sleeping. Sometimes problems disappear for awhile just because we have done something different, then as soon as things settle down, they rise up again. Part of following up on the solution includes finding out exactly how much it took to make the solution work. How much did it really cost? How much overtime, did we really put in that was directly related to our solution? Is the job actually *more* complicated as a result of our action?

These are fair questions to ask and we may need the information to support our next idea. If we have exceeded our estimated budget, it's a lot better for us to catch it than for someone else to. When we find out exactly what the costs were in terms of money, material and people, we can honestly answer the question, "Was it worth it?" This can only be done when all the facts and figures are in.

Review

Below are the problem-solving steps as they have been given:

Defining the problem
Gathering information
Finding the cause
Finding alternative solutions
Picking a solution
Putting the plan to work
Executing the plan
Following up on the solution

Chapter 12

In the beginning of this chapter we said that the process seems complicated. What we have tried to do is give the complete layout for an approach to problem-solving. It will be a rare day when we use each of these steps in its full extent. The idea is to see that the approach to problem-solving is systematic and not haphazard. Breaking it down into steps shows clearly that there is a beginning a middle and an end. The middle step is only one step, picking a solution. What comes before and after determines how well the solution we choose is going to work.

Chapter 13

Oral and Written Presentations

As managers, we find ourselves having to present solutions to problems we have solved or communicates our ideas up or down the line. We may do this by either speaking or writing. In either case, the acceptance of the message can depend as much on the quality of our writing or speaking as it does on the message itself. We can get poor results because we fail to do well at putting things in writing or speaking in front of people. Obviously, we can't become great writers or speakers overnight, but we can take a look at whet we're really trying to do when we write or speak.

Watch Stereotypes

Perhaps the most common mistake we make in trying to improve our writing or speaking is to assume that there is just one way to write or speak. We fail to realize that there are many acceptable ways to express ourselves. In

Chapter 13

writing, we can say things in several acceptable ways to reach our audience. We search for the correct form to use in a note or presentation and make the mistake that there is only one way to do it. If we stick to a stereotyped form in our writing, we may be stereotyping *ourselves*. We may convey that we have no imagination or that we are too formal, even when the situation calls for an informal approach.

Whether in speaking or writing, there is room for imagination, which means that the person who always says something a certain way or appears to be the perfect speaker, may not be the best *communicator*. In fact, the polished speaker will probably be out of place in the kind of speaking situations the manager gets into. There is just one standard for writing or speaking: *Get the message across*.

There is a three point plan of action that never fails. If we know these three things, we should be able to meet any kind of situation in which we are trying to get a message to someone else, whether by speaking or writing. They are:

Know your subject
Know your audience
Know yourself and your capabilities

Lets look at each of these and what they mean to us as managers.

Chapter 13

Know Your Subject

What does it mean to know the subject? It means we should research it until we are sure we have a complete understanding of what we are about to write or say.

Even if we aren't expected to be experts, we should at least know enough to see that our words and phrases are used correctly. This doesn't mean that we research something to death. It means that we simply learn as much as we are supposed to know – *maybe a little extra, but never a little less*. Of course, if we are looked on as an expert and others are looking to us for answers, then we need to do the additional research. Perhaps a better way to look at it is to know what is important and what is not.

Rather than becoming an expert on a whole subject, we figure out what part is important to the audience or the reader and focus on that. We may even have to educate the audience to the fact that certain things *are* important.

We also need to figure out what part is important to the project we're working on. Maybe the audience is interested in more information than the project requires or they think it would be interesting to pursue some things that really aren't related to it.

If so, we simply have to avoid the trap and get to the important points, even if our audience thinks they want something else. Of course, this means we must explain why we are leaving some things out and be prepared to defend our position.

We also need to be aware of ourselves and recognize that

Chapter 13

we sometimes may have pet projects that we like to discuss over and over again, so we have to learn to control ourselves as well.

One of the best ways the regulate ourselves and our audience is to be familiar with the subjects that relate to the one we're writing or speaking out. Not that we have to become experts – but just enough knowledge so we know how some of the related material might affect the outcome of the project being discussed, or so that we can answer some of the questions that might be asked later.

We shouldn't present ourselves as an expert. We should simply try to familiarize ourselves with enough of the information to give us a good idea of those things that relate to the project we are working on. Organization is the key, because as we begin to organize and tie up loose ends, we see where related subjects fit in and where the weak spots are.

Know Your Audience

Knowing your audience isn't as easy as it might appear. If, what we want them to have differs from what they think they need, then we've got to tell them *in terms that are meaningful to them*. Even though we're expressing our own thoughts and ideas on the subject, the way we express them must be in terminology the audience will understand.

Ideally, we should start off by making it clear that what the audience is getting what it asked for. This way the members are tuned it, whether they're getting the information exactly as they expected it or not. The way to

Chapter 13

appeal to the reader or listener is the same: "Here is the information you asked for." "You asked me to speak on..." We should always use the name of our reader or listener and use, *we* or *us*, instead of *I* or *me*. This helps keep it friendly and allows us to connect closer with our audience.

Know Yourself

The most important thing to know is, ourselves. What are our capabilities? If we have the ability to talk and write on a subject, we should use the opportunity to teach others and look good in the process.

We're writing or speaking because we know enough about the subject matter and it may offer a chance to showcase ourselves and that is an opportunity we should always take advantage of. We also have a chance to promote an idea or solution we have come up with.

If we have done the research, we should take the opportunity to sell it ourselves and not wait for someone else to explain it – a person who may not have all of the details or facts.

But we also need to know our limitations. Even if we're willing to make the speech or write the message, we should speak or write within our abilities. If we can't tell jokes effectively, we shouldn't try.

Use a substitute like a highlight from recent news reports or articles, or just play it straight. Whatever you choose, we should tell it simply, quickly and then stop when we

Chapter 13

are done. As we need to know our limitations, we also need to do something about them. We should be constantly striving to do better than the last time. If we feel that we didn't do too well, decide what we did wrong and then look for an opportunity to try to do better, not just stop with a failure.

Skillful communication is important to every manager. The ability to express yourself in writing or by speaking before a group is an asset that never goes out of style. At every level in the organization we are called upon to tell someone something. The *telling* is just as important as the *finding out what to tell*. Very few things will call attention to ourselves and to what we know, like the ability to say it or write it. A good oral recap or a crisp accurate report is a critical thing to those who are short on time and need to get their facts in a hurry. If we are able to provide them with this service, we will certainly be rewarded for it and the higher up we go in the organization, the more useful this skill becomes.

Tips on Writing

Generally there are just three reasons why we ever write anything: *to inform*, to *request* and to *verify or document*. When we write to inform, we are doing it because someone needs some information we have and has asked us to supply it, or we have information they should be using and we want them to have it. They may not know they need it, but at least we need to recognize that a particular message is for the purpose of giving someone some information. Writing to request information is quite different from writing to give information. Our approach is different in that we have to

Chapter 13

be more specific to get exactly what we need. Even in requesting information there are two reasons why we want it. First, we want it because we are going to use it; second, we want it because someone has asked us to get it for them. In the first case, we have only to determine exactly what we want and why we want it, then ask for it. In the second case, it's a little harder. We have a communication problem at both ends. We not only have to interpret someone else's needs and make sure we aren't asking for the wrong thing, but we also have to be sure what we are getting back is in a proper, usable form. This means we have the problem of deciding what the users are going to do with the information. If they are going to use it exactly as we have given it to put into their report, then we must ensure we give it to them in near final form.

If they're going to extract parts of the information and use it with other information, then we need to put it in a form that allows them to find things quickly. We need to communicate whichever need, to the people we are getting the information from which creates another communication challenge. The third reason for writing is to verify or document a conclusion or decision we have made. In this case we have to be sure to use all the rules of good communicating, because we are really in the selling business now. This is especially true if we are writing to verify someone else's idea or conclusion.

So we have three reasons for writing: to inform, to request and to verify or document. It's a simple thing to find out which reason we are writing for, but too many times we forget to do it. It's much easier to find the right words if we know why we are writing. It's also easier to

Chapter 13

proof-read our writing when we know exactly why we're writing in the first place. We say to ourselves, "Did I make it perfectly clear what I wanted, or does the reader have to guess?" "Did I spend so much time leading up to the subject that the reason for writing got lost?" It's always a good idea to put ourselves in the reader's position and see if we can decide what the message or report is all about. The simplest way to check our writing is to see if we got to the point quickly. It's just as bad to put in too much background as to put in too little. If we spend too much time leading up to the reason for writing, the reader may have left us before we get to it. The best way is to open up with the purpose of the message.

"Here is the answer on the forming machine you requested..."

"Can you tell us how many of these you will need in the next month"

"We recommend canceling the project immediately..."

With lead-in sentences like these, the reader won't have to guess why we are writing the letter or report. We spare the details until we have established our reason for writing, but we also need to get to the point quickly. We don't use obscure words or phrases that are only familiar to us or our organization. We state the purpose early; we don't bury it between background detail and unimportant information. The reader should be able to tell at a glance what he or she is supposed to do. All of this comes early and clearly in the report. Any supporting data comes at the end of the report or as an attachment to the note.

Chapter 13

To learn to write, we must write, we must practice, re-read whatever we've written, then practice some more. We should read other people's writings and reports and analyze them. We should ask ourselves why they worded them as they did, admit to the good things they have done – *then imitate the good things.* Most good writers readily admit they started out by imitating those people who were already successful, so there's no shame in recognizing and copying good writing style. If there are people in the organization who have a reputation for good writing, study what they have written, see what it is that makes their material precise and easy to read – then try to do the same.

Tips on Speaking

One can't learn to speak well just by reading about it, but there are some things to look for and to do that will improve our ability as speakers if we take advantage of the knowledge we have gained. We must learn to *practice, practice, practice.* We don't have to practice every word we are going to say, but we need to work on phrases and try different combinations of words in order to get the most out of the words we use. Since we're more likely to be nervous at the beginning, we should practice our opening remarks until they're as precise as we can make them. If we make a good start, the rest will comes easy. Our confidence will be higher and the audience reception will be better. Another way to build our confidence is to try out our ideas on other people. We shouldn't expect them to listen to our entire speech, but we should at least get them to react to our key points and

Chapter 13

ideas. Do they understand what we are saying? Do they see the logic we're using? Do they have some good arguments for why we should say it differently?

When we start to speak, we must be alert to the audience's reaction. Do they look receptive? Are they bored? Is there anyone in the group that looks friendly and appears to be nodding their head in agreement? If so, it will build our confidence to direct our attention to him or her frequently to see how we're doing. Be careful though, as this person may not a good gauge of the thinking and feeling of the entire audience. One way to keep the audience with us is to get feedback from them. Look them in the eye when we have made a good point and try to get them to nod, smile or frown. Don't be afraid to ask them to raise their hand if they agree or disagree with a point of the discussion. This way we've made it clear that we're talking *to* and *with* them, not just *at* them. Look around the group and don't just talk to one side of the room or to a few people in the front row.

There's nothing wrong with using notes, in fact, the audience expects it. But notes are just notes, they're not our entire speech written out. Very few people can write out their whole speech then make it look casual and natural. If our notes are not much shorter than the speech, then we're really just going to end up reading the speech. If so, then why not just send everyone in the audience a copy of your speech and save them some time? The rule for making notes is *to put only the key points and phrases on them plus any statistics or figures we need to remember*. Practice will also reduce the need for notes.

Chapter 13

One thing that will help us eliminate the need for notes is to have some good speaking aids. This will add another dimension to our speaking and one we have to be careful that we don't misuse. The trouble is that we tend to use things such as visuals, flipcharts, white boards and Powerpoint as crutches rather than aids. We depend on them to help *us*, not the audience. Just because we can get a lot of figures on a projected visual doesn't mean the audience is going to remember it all or give it their attention for very long. There's nothing exciting about looking a screen full of statistics for several minutes while a speaker reads and comments on them. If the aid doesn't make the point any clearer, don't use it. But some aids are critical. There isn't a better way to show a relationship of parts to the whole than to use a pie chart or similar type of charts. *We remember what we see much longer than what we hear*, so good visuals can save us a lot of words if we use them effectively.

Review

A final tip for those of us who find ourselves in the situation of having to write something or speak before a group of any size: *be friendly on purpose*. Write and speak with a smile. Let our writing show we are friendly by our use of people's names. Refer to things that the readers are familiar with, rather than examples that only relate to our experience. The same is true for our speaking. Happiness is contagious. We can get away with a lot by saying things in a friendly way. This will come easier as we speak and write more and to do our job well, we must steadily develop these skills.

Chapter 14

Self-Development and Evaluation

New and emerging managers need to know how and where to develop themselves. As we get busy in the everyday problems of the job, we forget to look at ourselves to see if we are any better at our work than we were a few months ago. In fact, we probably forgot what areas we were supposed to improve in. Little problems seem like big ones when they are with us, so we spend all of our time worrying about them and fail to realize that good managers have to think about the future as well as the present. Not only do we need to worry about the long range objectives of the organization, *we need to think about some long range objectives for ourselves.*

We shouldn't spend all of our time worrying about our next big promotion; we simply have to realize that we really aren't going to be of much value to the organization if we fail to grow to our full potential. But how do we develop ourselves and what are the areas that get the most attention? The answers to these questions will make

Chapter 14

the difference in where we will be in ten years from now and what we will be doing then.

How Do We Develop

How can we improve ourselves if we have all the problems of the job to worry about? The chances are that we are going to be so busy we can't take time away to train ourselves or even do much planning about the future – *and here we have the first indicator that we need some development.* If we can't get the job done in the time allotted to us and also can't find time to look at next week and next year, we may need to look at the way we are doing our job. Are we really organized in our work effort?

Are we spinning our wheels doing things that should be delegated to others? Are we doing things over because they weren't done correctly the first time? Are we spending too much time on small, insignificant details while letting other problems grow bigger? There some obvious signs to show us how well we are doing. Let's see what we can do about some of them.

First, consider the matter of not having enough time. One sign that we aren't utilizing our efforts very well is that we're working without a plan. It's a challenging cycle, because the less time we have, the less we plan and the less we plan, the more time it takes do the job and we run out of time.

This goes on and on until we finally discover ourselves overwhelmed with work and no time to plan it. The results are that we aren't very efficient at our job and may

Chapter 14

overlook the things we should be doing. One way to turn this process around is to stop the cycle. We can start this by taking five minutes at the start of the day to try to put things in order. If we don't do this, we'll probably do the first thing that comes up whether it's important or not. Five minutes of deciding what needs to be done first and what can wait will save us from falling behind in our day.

Another five minutes will allow us to decide what *we* need to handle and *what we can delegate* to some one else. Another issue we need to watch for as managers, is our tendency to more and more of our employees' job ourselves..."because I can do it in less time than it takes to explain or train someone else." When we get into this cycle, we're doing more and our people are doing less.

They're not happy because they see us doing work that they could and should be doing. We're unhappy because we're doing work we shouldn't be doing and may even decide that our people are lazy or unmotivated because they aren't doing more – *all because we haven't taken to time to plan our work very well.*

Remember, these are indicators we need to develop; they're not cures. The matter of how we develop is just as important.

So far, we've seen that one way is to force ourselves to do five or ten minutes of planning and delegating. Another way is to give ourselves some 'instant success.' We need confidence in ourselves and this comes from accomplishing something. Even if the thing isn't the biggest or most important job we've ever done, just finishing a task will boost our confidence a lot. How can

Chapter 14

we use this technique to our advantage? One simple method is to make a list of things we have to accomplish in a period of time: a day, a week or two weeks. We list the things on a page and then number them according to priority. As we accomplish them we mark as completed, this way we can see what we have accomplished. When we see we have gotten some additional things completed during the course of a busy day we will start to build our confidence. The next day or at the end of the day, we make a new list, deleting the completed items and adding and prioritizing new items for the upcoming day. Two things become very obvious as we follow this procedure:

One is that it shows us how much we really are doing and the other is that it gives us an opportunity to plan, organize and prioritize our work.

As we see the things we have to do, we may see some duplication of effort. We may see that someone in the office can do two or three of the items because of the close relation between them. Also, as we list the things to be done, we have a chance to set some priorities. Obviously we want to do the important things first, so they should be near the top of the list. Getting the right size list is also important. If we can organize the large tasks into small logical, prioritized steps we will do a better overall job and will achieve frequent successes.

Another way we can develop is to watch others. First we watch our boss or someone else who is getting a lot of work done in the same amount of time we're working. We study their behavior, their patterns and their organizing. We try to figure out what it is that makes them able to get so much done or even *briefly* discuss the matter with them. They probably get a lot of work done because they make good use of their time and we don't want to be guilty of taking too much of their time with our poor organizational habits. The way to discuss the subject is by asking the right questions, not be asking them to solve our problems. We watch people work, then ask them why they did certain things. "Why did you call that meeting?" "What was the advantage to calling the meeting?" Of course, we need to be completely clear that we aren't questioning their wisdom we're just trying to improve on our own.

To improve on our perception, we can try to anticipate what their answers will be. We try to figure out the reasoning they give. As we get closer, we can see that our judgment is getting better. We're probably making better decisions on our own job now.

Next we make an effort to judge the abilities of our people. We see how well they accept the responsibilities we give them and make an effort to give them more as they are able to handle them. We aren't just trying to get more work out of them; we're trying to expand their ability to handle more important assignments.

Appraising others isn't the easiest thing to do and neither is delegating. Our ability to do these together is one of the measures of success we can use. There are those who fear giving up responsibility and authority to those under them. Some fear that those under them will somehow get the credit and maybe take their job. Such lack of confidence in oneself is a sign or poor leadership and immaturity. One of the common traits of most good leaders is that they surround themselves with people who

Chapter 14

will assume responsibility when it is given. We should keep this is mind when we consider whether we should let someone else do the some of the work or make some of the decisions. Others fear giving up any responsibility and authority due to fear that if the job is done wrong, they will have to assume the blame. The truth is, that's the whole point – good leaders are willing to take the blame to protect the people under us and continue to give them the confidence to take the necessary risks until they have convinced themselves that can do the job.

This doesn't mean that we are going to let think that everything went well. It means that we will be the buffer between them and higher management. It means that that we will know and tell them if they did the job well or poorly, but for a while they are safe under our protection.

Once they feel this, they should respond with good, creative decision making. If we don't create this type of atmosphere, we will be stuck with the work ourselves and the continued problem of not having enough time for our job.

Personal Development

There is more to developing than just becoming better on the job. We need to make ourselves better in our lives. This includes becoming more informed on what's going on in our community, in the world and in our profession. It includes becoming readers and writers.

We need to better relate to the world so we can relate to our people, who will come from various backgrounds and cultures. How do we do these things? We do it by making

Chapter 14

an effort to be better. Let's look at some things that will help.

First, we need to do some self analysis, by measuring our abilities and shortcomings. We need to decide what we do well, what we do poorly and what we can't do at all. We need to decide what we like to do, what we don't like to do and where we have the possibility of getting better.

Next, after we've taken a realistic look at ourselves we need to look at our biases and mental blocks. Do we find ourselves hesitant at the thought of presenting something in front of the group then decide that we really don't have to do it anyway? Do we hate to read then say to ourselves that we can learn more by watching television? Do we dislike writing reports then console ourselves by deciding that we will never be able to write because we don't have the gift or writing? These are all biases that, if not overcome, will hurt us in the long run.

Having looked at our likes and dislikes and determined that we need to improve on some of the things we don't like to do, we take the next step of setting our priorities.

We decide what we want to improve on in one of several ways. We determine which one is the most valuable to us in our job or family or which one will help us the most in doing the things we need or want to do.

We can decide which we're the worst at, or which will take us the longest to develop a skill for. We can see which one will be the easiest for us to develop, giving us a quicker boost when we start our 'redevelopment' program.

Chapter 14

Whatever project we decide for ourselves, we need to set some goals and make some realistic plans for accomplishing these goals. It is not enough to say, "I'm going to get better at this during the next six months," without saying how much better or how we're going to get better. Let's look at some specific things we can improve on, some of the things that people in general are weak on and some things we've already mentioned. Take writing, for example. Many people hate to write and don't feel they're good at it. But all of us need to be able to write satisfactorily if we ever expect to do our job well. So how do we learn to write? We find that people who force themselves to write, even if they are frequent emails to friends or family, get better at it, especially if they go back and read what they've written before they send the letter.

Another way to improve our writing is to study what others have written. If we work for someone we think writes well, we should study carefully samples of that person's notes and memos. The idea isn't to copy somebody's style, but to see what makes them good writers. We should study a letter, memo or report until we see what they're doing that we are failing to do. Maybe it's not more than short sentences. Maybe they're picking simple precise words. Maybe they're limiting the length of their paragraphs. Whatever it is, we can see that they're doing something we aren't.

It we're serious about writing better, we can even take a course to help us. There are seminars or short courses that will take no more than a few days and should help teach us what we need to know for better writing. The advantage of taking a course is that we get pointed in the right way, so we'll be practicing the correct things rather

Chapter 14

then making the same mistakes we now make. If we don't take a course, at least we can *read*. Reading will help us to improve in all kinds of ways, including our writing.

Let's look at another area in which we may need to improve. Suppose we have decided to get over our fear of public speaking. We have convinced ourselves that we have as much to say as any other manager in the organization, but we don't have the confidence to get up and talk, even in a small, informal meeting. What can we do?

There are many places we can get training on public speaking, but no matter where we go, or who trains us, the main thing is that we'll have to speak before a group eventually. It's like driving a car; we can read books and watch videos on the subject, but we won't learn to drive until we get behind the wheel and get on the road. It will be hard the first time, the second time, the third time and maybe even several more times; but it will get easier each time.

We have talked about broadening our perspective about things around us. How do we do that? The answer most people offer, is *reading*. If nothing else comes from reading, we can make ourselves more disciplined by taking time every day to read something that has some value in it. There are those who are successful in business because they forced themselves to read something they otherwise wouldn't have read. There is some value in that.

Try reading a magazine or article that doesn't sound interesting. Read it for ten minutes and it may surprise us

Chapter 14

to find that we actually learned something and maybe use that information in a conversation one day soon.

We can learn to read better by reading more. Not only will we become better readers, but we will also be better informed and better disciplined readers.

The Next Job

There are two reasons for developing ourselves – to do better in our present jobs, and to be ready for our next one. It is important to keep them in this order – the present job, *then* the next one. This may sound simple enough, but many good managers fail to get promoted because they get so interested in the next job that they forget to deal properly with the present one.

The first thing that happens is that our interest begins to slip. An important assignment gets too little attention. Details are overlooked and wrong decisions are made. Errors start growing and higher management gets involved to find out what happened. Now we may find that someone in higher management is starting to doubt our ability and may be lose out on new opportunities in the future.

Some have said, "Do well on the present assignment, and the future will take care of itself." That's good advice, but it doesn't include all that is necessary to get ahead. It assumes that the things that are needed on the next job are already in the present one. This is may not be true. If the next level above us requires considerable report writing and we don't think we are very good at it, this is one area to focus on.

Chapter 14

We can look around for places to learn more about report writing and we can look for opportunities to do some report writing in our present job. We can start by making short reports on things the boss has asked us for then work up to longer and more complex ones. Just doing reports is good place to learn, but we should also do some studying and developing on our own. We follow the same routine in the other areas where we think the next job exceed our present requirements.

The advantage of this approach is that it will actually make us look better on our present assignment, rather than like we have abandoned any interest in it. While we are improving in our existing job and improving our reputation, we are also preparing ourselves to take on a more responsible task when the opportunity arises.

One final word about the next job: Most successful people will tell us that they got the job by being in the right place at the right time *and* by being ready for when the occasion arose. We have to develop ourselves to take over the added responsibility but also have the present one covered.

Successful managers will be sensitive to their own needs for development and will always find the ways to make the necessary improvements. Most likely they will see this as a challenge and make it happen. Good managerial skills can be learned. If we take the time to tep back and really look at ourselves, we'll see that we have already come a long way. It may have been hard work on the journey, but the rest of the trip will be even better.

Review

We've already said that appraising our people is hard job. A much harder job is to *appraise ourselves*. Looking objectively at our own strengths and weaknesses is almost impossible for most of us, but if we're going to improve ourselves, we have to be willing to see both the good and the bad in ourselves. We look at things like time management, delegation, training, communication, interpersonal skills and imagine that we are appraising ourselves. We look for a standard then measure our performance against that same standard.

If we really are serious about becoming effective managers we need to set some goal for ourselves and decide what we must overcome in reaching them. If we look at ourselves and decide that getting to a certain goal is out of reach at this time, then we set another short range goal and go for it. If we decide that there are things in the way that are out of our power to control, then we set another goal.

The key is to set a goal and then direct our energies toward getting there, remembering that the majority of the successes we have, aren't because of someone else; they're because of us. We don't need anyone pulling us in the organization to get ahead we just need a push from within ourselves.

We have now reached the end of our journey in learning how to be an *effective manager*. We have tried to lay out the opportunities for strong growth and development, but this is not to suggest that everything in this book is applicable to every new and advancing manager. The suggestions are just that – suggestions. The manager will be no worse for having considered them, but hopefully will get a new idea to help in solving his or her problems.

If the suggestions and resulting ideas pay off, then it will have been a great investment of your time to have read this book.

Epilogue

This isn't a rule book; it's a *guide book*. You may choose to read this book in stages or re-read certain sections to gain a better understanding and make notes on each page as a reference. The ideas and suggestions in this book have all been tried in some shape or form by many successful managers. Whether or not they work for you is not a measure of your effectiveness or your abilities; but its proof that managing people is complex and deserves all of our efforts and skills. If we are willing to put all of our energies into the job and are willing to learn the skills, then there can only be one result – we will end up being *effective managers*. There may be better rewards, but this one will last throughout our careers.

Index

Index

Index

Index